TEXAS

DO YOUR OWN NONPROFIT

ALSO BY DR. KITTY BICKFORD:

This is book 43 of the 51 book
Do Your Own Nonprofit state series.

Nonprofit Touchdown:
Winning the 501(c) (3) Game Against IRS.

TEXAS

DO YOUR OWN NONPROFIT

The ONLY GPS You Need for

501(c)(3) Tax Exempt Approval

DR. KITTY BICKFORD, DBS
FOUNDER, PASTURE VALLEY CHILDREN MISSIONS

CHALFANT ECKERT

PUBLISHING

ISBN-13: 978-1-63308-090-4 (paperback journal edition)
ISBN-10: 1633080900 (paperback journal edition)
ISBN-13: 978-1-63308-091-1 (ebook)
ISBN-10: 1633080919 (ebook)

Cover Design by R'tor John D. Maghuyop
Interior Design by R'tor John D. Maghuyop

CHALFANT ECKERT
PUBLISHING

1028 S Bishop Avenue, Dept. 178
Rolla, MO 65401

www.doyourownnonprofit.com

Printed in the United States of America

To Fellow Texans

James and Betty Robison

Whose Mission Feeding and Water for LIFE programs show

Christ's love in action. When I founded Pasture Valley Children

Missions, it was their example I strived to emulate.

TABLE OF CONTENTS

PART I
PRELIMINARY ORGANIZATIONAL SET UP

PART II
IRS FORM 1023 APPLICATION
FOR TAX EXEMPT STATUS

PART III
SPECIAL CIRCUMSTANCES

PART IV
OPTIONAL FOLLOW UP TASKS

FOREWORD

How does one respond when someone you greatly admire asks you to pen a foreword for her latest effort? You check to make sure the email was sent to the correct address, of course! Dr. Bickford is a gem. On the surface, she's all no-nonsense; spit and polish. And this comes through in her excellent writing. Yet she's also one of the kindest and most gracious women you will ever meet. She's passionate about her love of God, passionate about caring for her family, and passionate about loving her neighbors. And those neighbors are in Rolla, MO and around the globe!

My wife, Sarah, first introduced me to Dr. Bickford after a speaking engagement at a local women's conference. Over a slice of pie, Dr. Bickford recounted her story of Swaziland. It was absolutely fascinating. Faced with the surprise that her original charity of choice wasn't delivering on its promises, Dr. Bickford began to use her financial resources to partner with folks one-on-one. But she didn't stop there. Dr. Bickford also used her skills as an Air Force instructor and public school teacher to set-up her own non-profit. Along the way, she solved many of the problems faced by those attempting to tackle complex paperwork with minimal assistance from (sometimes costly) legal professionals. And this book is the culmination of her efforts.

I like to think of Dr. Bickford's writing as an easy to follow 'cookbook'. Mix the proper ingredients, in the proper proportions, and bake for the proper time. In these step-by-step chapters she lays out everything that's needed to set up a successful Non Governmental Organization (NGO), and her writing is clear and straightforward. My wife, Sarah, and I are fans of Dr. Bickford's work. We've met many times with the Bickfords, sharing pieces of pie and discussing how to make the world a better place for our neighbors. We are pleased to offer modest financial support to folks in Swaziland through a partnership with Pasture Valley Children Missions, but perhaps even more importantly we are proud of the exceptional work of our good friend.

Please enjoy this book, and keep pushing forward with your own goals for establishing a 501 (c) (3). The work is worth the effort for those you serve!

Daniel B. Oerther, PhD, PE, BCEE
John A. and Susan Mathes Chair of Environmental Engineering
Missouri University of Science and Technology
Rolla, MO
April, 2014

ACKNOWLEDGMENTS

I especially want to thank God for His marvelous direction in my life. I never know what will come next, and each new adventure He sends me on is better than the last, and much more exciting than I could have dreamed up on my own. I am deeply grateful to my family and friends who encouraged me during the writing of this 51-book series. Without your support and belief in me, I might not have attempted this project.

DISCLAIMER

While the information contained in this book was prepared with best efforts and in good faith, the publisher and author make no representations or warranties with respect to the accuracy or completeness of the contents herein.

This work (in any electronic or digital form or in any other printed material form) is not intended for use as a source of legal, accounting, tax, or financial advice. If advice concerning legal, accounting, tax, financial, or any other professional advice is needed, the services of a qualified, properly licensed and competent professional should be sought.

The contents of this work reflect the views and opinions of the author. The author and publisher have made their best effort to produce a high quality, informative and helpful course on getting approved for Section 501(c) (3) status by the Internal Revenue Service (IRS). But they make no representation or warranties of any kind with regard to the completeness and accuracy of the contents of the course. Any slights of people and/or organizations are unintentional.

Neither the author nor the publisher accept any liability of any kind for any losses or damages caused or alleged to be caused, directly or indirectly, from using the information contained in this book. Every individual must make his or her own decisions. Although this book describes the experiences of the author, it in no way guarantees similar success for others. Every effort has been made to ensure that this publication is free from errors and/or problems.

ABOUT THE AUTHOR

MILITARY CAREER AND FAMILY

Dr. Kitty Bickford is a Christian woman who spent from 1979–1989 in the United States Air Force. The last five years of her military career were spent as a Master Instructor and On-the-Job Training Advisor for Air Training Command, achieving the noncommissioned officer rank of E-6, Technical Sergeant.

In 1984, she met and eventually married Master Sergeant Jim Bickford who was twenty two years her senior. They have been happy together for over thirty years, enjoying four children, fourteen grandchildren (one with God), and two great grandsons.

TEACHING AND MISSIONARY WORK

After leaving the military, Kitty continued her teaching career, first teaching college, then teaching public school. She has taught Family and Consumer Science at Rolla Middle School in Rolla, Missouri, since 2004 and holds lifetime teaching certifications in nine curriculums. She serves on the Board of Directors for Kid Care America/Thrive Student Centers, an after school program for at-risk children hosted by the Assemblies of God church. Jim and Kitty spend their Spring breaks and summers doing mission work from Dillingham, Alaska to Swaziland, Africa.

In 2006, Kitty was selected as ING Corporation's Unsung Hero for Missouri for educational innovation. She has made over 225 microfinance loans to the world's poor through Kiva.org, mostly disadvantaged women. These loans allow women to start their own businesses and become self-sufficient.

She supports missionaries to Zimbabwe, Botswana, Zambia, and Ukraine. She was awarded the 2013 Spirit of Rolla Award in recognition of significant achievement and/or lifetime contribution to the spirit of giving. She holds undergraduate degrees in Educational Administration, Behavioral Science, and Criminal Justice, completed the undergraduate teacher certification program for Missouri, holds a graduate degree in Psychology, has studied Special Education at the doctorate level, and holds a Doctorate in Biblical Studies.

PHILANTHROPY

In 2005, Kitty sponsored an orphaned child in Swaziland, Africa. When she went to visit him in 2012, she was disappointed to find that the organization she trusted to care for him lacked the integrity she expected. Upon returning to the United States, God led her to start a nonprofit organization that would not be corrupt and would actually do some good for hungry kids and vulnerable families.

The 501(c) (3) process is either long and complicated, or very expensive. Kitty chose the long and complicated option because spending up to $7,000 on an attorney to do paperwork seemed counterproductive to her. After much study, questioning, and hard work, the organization she started was approved by IRS on the first try. Elated, she thanked God that the process was over so she could get down to work feeding children. To her surprise, God spoke to her spirit and told her to write a book for others who want to start a nonprofit on a shoestring. She wrote *Nonprofit Touchdown: Winning the 501(c) (3) Game Against IRS.* It was 370 pages long, a national edition that covered all 50 states and DC. She later decided that smaller, more compact state guides would be easier for the reader to use. That is where this and 50 other similar publications in the series came from. They are miniature versions of the bigger national book.

PART I

PRELIMINARY ORGANIZATIONAL SET UP

CHAPTER 1

IS A 501(C) (3) THE RIGHT CHOICE?

"Twenty years from now you will be more disappointed by the things that you didn't do than by the ones you did do."

—Mark Twain

Pasture Valley Children Missions *was founded by Dr. Kitty Bickford to provide a hand up, not a hand out, to orphans and vulnerable families in Swaziland, Africa.*

STEP BY STEP INSTRUCTIONS

So you have this great idea for a nonprofit floating around in your head, but just don't know what to do with it. If so, you are not alone. Many people want to make a difference in the world, but they either don't know how, can't afford an attorney to set it up, or they get buried in the mountain of paperwork needed to get 501(c) (3) tax exempt status.

It is my desire to be a one woman battering ram to knock down the doors that don't want to open for you. I know from personal experience the areas that give a lot of grief, so much so that many people give up because it is just too hard.

This book gives you step by step instructions of what to do in the correct order for your state, how to do it, where to do it, how long it takes, who to call, and what it costs. Just that information saves much time and aggravation. But that is not all you get.

ASK ME 3 SPECIFIC QUESTIONS

You get to ask me three specific questions during your 501(c) (3) project. It is my way of saying thank you for buying my book. Just go to www.doyourownnonprofit.com and contact me. I am glad to help you! But that is not all. I have gone the extra mile and given you great resources I wish I would have had that will remove the most frustrating part of the tax exempt process: paperwork!

FILL IN THE BLANK STATE TEMPLATES

Does the thought of preparing articles of organization, bylaws, conflict of interest policies, and board meeting minutes make you nervous? Your stomach queasy? Fill you with dread? Make you want to forget the whole idea?

I had the same feelings when I started Pasture Valley Children Missions, so when I started this series of books, I hired a $300 an hour attorney on your behalf to develop fill in the blank templates of all your state documents. All you have to do is pay a small fee to download them, fill in the blanks, print and mail. Now you can do the state paperwork in 30 minutes instead of 30 days, with full assurance of legal integrity of the documents.

EXAMPLES OF APPROVED NONPROFITS

A picture is worth a thousand words, so I researched other 501(c) (3) organizations and in Appendix A you will find links to their paperwork. These links are also live on the book website. Find an organization like the one you are starting and study their federal application before filling out yours.

I hope that the benefits of the book, website, templates, and access to paperwork from other nonprofits makes your experience easy and trouble-free. And I hope you will contact me if you run into trouble so we can figure it out together. Once you receive your determination letter from IRS, contact me at www.doyourownnonprofit.com and I will publicize your cause on my website. Now let's look at the benefits of starting a tax exempt organization.

BENEFITS OF 501(C) (3) STATUS

People pursue 501(c) (3) status for different reasons. In addition to the intangible rewards (satisfaction, doing the right thing, helping people, feeling good about your efforts), there are tangible reasons to pursue your mission as a tax exempt organization.

Below are a few of the more tangible benefits:

- Tax deductions to contributors
- Limited liability
- Perpetual existence and permanence
- Eligibility for grants
- Tax exempt purchasing power in some states
- Reduced postage

- Discounted internet service provider costs
- Public service announcements on the radio and other media at little or no charge

Getting to the approval process with the Internal Revenue Service (IRS) requires many steps be completed along the way. This state guide is designed to get you there quickly with no unnecessary steps, wasted effort, or scratching your head wondering what to do next. The best part is that you do not have to hire an attorney to do the paperwork for you. If you can follow a checklist, you can complete the requirements to get tax exempt status.

IRS states that for an organization to be tax exempt, it must be "organized and operated exclusively for exempt purposes set forth in Section 501(c) (3)..."

Those exempt purposes include:

- Charitable
- Religious
- Educational
- Scientific
- Literary
- Testing for public safety (although contributions are not tax deductible)
- Fostering national or international sports competition
- Preventing cruelty to children and animals

IRS DIRECTIVE

Here's how the IRS looks at the status:

> ... the term charitable is used in its generally accepted legal sense and includes relief of the poor, the distressed, or the underprivileged; advancement of religion; advancement of education or science; erecting or maintaining public buildings, monuments, or works;

lessening the burdens of government; lessening neighborhood tensions; eliminating prejudice and discrimination; defending human and civil rights secured by law; and combating community deterioration and juvenile delinquency.

CHURCHES AND RELIGIOUS ENTITIES

Religious nonprofits are harder to pinpoint, but form a class of exemption with some commonalities. If it looks like a church, acts like a church, operates like a church, and feels like a church, then it is probably a church. However, a church must have:

- distinct religious beliefs
- a location to meet
- a schedule of services on a regular basis
- a stable group of people that make up the congregation

Proof of these things may be required to get the exemption. IRS defines church to also include synagogues, temples, and mosques.

In the list below are those that do not have to file the 501(c) (3) application as they are automatically exempt:

- Churches
- Interchurch organizations of the local units of the church
- Conventions or associations of churches
- Integrated auxiliaries of a church (such as a men's or women's organization)
- Religious school
- Mission society
- Youth group

That being said, many churches still choose to file because it assures their donors that contributions qualify for tax deductions. Church auxiliary organizations can fall under the umbrella of the church for

501(c) (3) purposes under certain circumstances. The benefit of being under that umbrella is that there is no requirement to file an annual return with IRS.

Many other religious organizations that are not churches under IRS codes, may still qualify for tax exempt status as religious organizations. These might include:

- Mission organizations
- Speakers' organizations
- Nondenominational ministries
- Ecumenical organizations
- Faith-based social agencies

Each of the above may fulfill the intent of religious exemption and therefore be granted 501(c) (3) status by IRS.

EDUCATIONAL ORGANIZATIONS

The IRS definition of educational organizations include schools at all levels from elementary to college, as well as trade schools, correspondence schools, and schools that provide education through media such as TV or radio. Some other types of organizations that may not be immediately obvious as educational may qualify:

- Museums
- Zoos
- Planetariums
- Symphony orchestras
- Organizations that conduct public discussion groups, forums, panels, and lectures.

In addition, nonprofit day care centers and youth sports organizations may qualify as educational tax exempt organizations.

SCIENTIFIC ORGANIZATIONS

Scientific organizations that want 501(c) (3) status must demonstrate that their research is in the public interest. This is done by using the results (including patents, copyrights, processes, or formulas) in a nondiscriminatory way for the public good. The research can be for science education, publication available to the public, curing disease, or to help attract new industry to an area. Research does not include product testing.

LITERARY ORGANIZATIONS

Literary organizations seeking 501(c) (3) status must be able to show that any sales or publishing they do is related to their tax exempt purpose.

AMATEUR ATHLETIC ORGANIZATIONS

Amateur Athletic organizations fall into two categories:

1. Those that promote national or international amateur sports competition but do not supply facilities or equipment
2. Those that exclusively develop athletes and/or conduct national or international amateur sports competition and provide facilities and equipment, even though the membership is local or regional.

ORGANIZATIONS THAT PREVENT CRUELTY TO CHILDREN AND ANIMALS

Organizations that seek to prevent cruelty to children and animals may:

- Try to protect children forced in dangerous jobs
- Advocate alternatives to child abuse

- Seek humane treatment for laboratory animals
- Assist in animal population control
- Provide shelters for abused animals
- Other attempts to positively impact cruelty to animals or children

SEPARATE ENTITY FROM FOUNDERS

Your organization must be set up and organized in such a way that IRS recognizes it as a separate entity from its founders. In other words, the people who start it do not own it. It is not their organization; it is separate and perpetual and will survive even if the founders do not. For this reason, be careful not to set yourself as an owner of a 501(c) (3) organization. You can start it, you can be on the board, you can be president of the board, you can be an advisor, but you *cannot be an owner*. A tax exempt organization is NOT owned. It is not operated by one individual, it is normally governed and run by a board of directors, and there are distinct rules about the number and relationships of those on the board (covered in a later chapter).

NOT FOR PRIVATE INTEREST

Section 501(c) (3) status DOES NOT apply to organizations created for the benefit of private interests or those that do not receive a substantial part of their income from the general public or the government. You cannot get 501(c) (3) status so that you or your family or friends can benefit from the tax exempt status. It must be public to be eligible for 501(c) (3). Your organization also cannot be set up to benefit a specific person or organization. You cannot participate in political campaigns directly or indirectly at any level, but you can have educational meetings, create educational materials, and appear before government bodies. You may not participate in illegal activities.

Now that you know the basic nonprofit categories, let's get you organized with a checklist so you can track your progress as you make it.

CHAPTER 2

DO-IT-YOURSELF CHECKLIST

*"Every great dream begins with a dreamer. Always remember,
you have within you the strength, the patience, and the passion to
reach for the stars to change the world."*

—Harriet Tubman

Francis of Assisi said that you eat an elephant one bite at a time, so before you become overwhelmed with the process, just concentrate on taking the bite in front of you, and when you swallow that requirement, go on to the next bite. You will be surprised how quickly you can devour the whole proverbial elephant and form a nonprofit corporation that is state and federally recognized. Each chapter of this book is written in this specific order to help you do the required steps in the right order the first time.

PRELIMINARY SET UP

_____ Determine the tax exempt purpose

      _____ charitable

      _____ religious

      _____ educational

      _____ scientific

      _____ literary

      _____ testing for public safety

      _____ fostering sports competition

_____ preventing cruelty to children

_____ preventing cruelty to animals

_____ Select and reserve business name with the state

_____ Get a Federal Employer Identification Number (FEIN)

_____ Develop a strong mission statement

_____ Form a board of directors

_____ **Prepare Certificate of Formation

_____ **Prepare Bylaws

_____ **Develop Conflict of Interest Policy

_____ **Hold and document the first board meeting

Go to **www.doyourownnonprofit.com for attorney developed fill-in-the-blank state compliant document templates containing all required IRS language, making a month long paperwork mountain into a 30 minute job. You can thank me later! **

COMPLETE IRS FORM 1023: APPLICATION FOR TAX EXEMPTION

_____ Part I, Identification of Applicant

_____ Part II, Organizational Structure

_____ Part III, Provisions in your Documents

_____ Part IV, Narrative Description of Your Activities

_____ Part V, Compensation and Other Financial Arrangements

_____ Part VI, Your Members and Other Individuals and Organizations That Receive Benefits from You

_____ Part VII, Your History

_____ Part VIII, Specific Activities

_____ Part IX, Financial Data

_____ Part X, Public Charity Status and any required schedules

      _____ Part X, Schedules A, B, C, and D

      _____ Part X, Schedule E: Organizations Not Filing Form 1023 within 27 Months of Formation

      _____ Part X, Schedules F, G, and H

_____ Part XI, User Fee Information

FOLLOW UP TASKS:

_____ Register for charitable fundraising and solicitation

_____ Know what annual filings are required by IRS, and when they are due

_____ Submit PS Form 3624, *Application to Mail at Nonprofit Standard Mail Rates*

CHAPTER 3

SELECT A BUSINESS NAME AND RESERVE IT WITH THE STATE

"The difference between the impossible and the possible lies in a man's determination."

—Tommy Lasorda

SELECT NAME AND DESIGNATE SUFFIX

Are you setting up a trust, unincorporated association, or a corporation? Most nonprofits are corporations because founders have the most personal protection from law suits and other legal matters, and the nonprofit is eligible for more grants than other forms of organization.

Don't let the designation *corporation* scare you, it can start small and stay small, or start small and grow huge. That depends on what you do to grow it. But first you must have a unique name, different from all other business and organization names in Texas. Also be careful not to pick something too close to well-known nonprofits, even if they are in another state. Very similar names can cause confusion, and claims of infringement from the other nonprofit. Spend some time thinking about what your organization represents and come up with a name that fits what you plan to do. In Texas, you are not required to add a designation suffix to the name (such as Corporation, Incorporated, Inc., or Corp.), it is your choice. You must choose your designation in the paperwork you file, but it doesn't have to be in the name.

CHECK NAME AVAILABILITY
AND RESERVE IF DESIRED

Next you must check with the Secretary of State's office and find out if the name is available. You do not have to reserve the name in Texas, but you can for up to 120 days if you want to. It costs $40, so unless you are worried about someone nabbing the name right from under your nose, you may just want to skip name reservation. The name will be yours when you file your Certificate of Formation.

If you go to my website, www.doyourownnonprofit.com and click on the *Helpful Links* tab, you will find a link to check the name and reserve it if you wish. Otherwise you can call the Secretary of State Corporations Division at (512) 475-2755. You can also sosdirect@ sos.texas.gov

Now that you have decided what to call your nonprofit, your next step will be to get a Federal Employer Identification Number. Details follow in the next chapter.

CHAPTER 4

GET A FEDERAL EMPLOYER IDENTIFICATION NUMBER (FEIN)

"What you finish is more important than what you begin."

—Mike Murdock

FEDERAL EMPLOYER IDENTIFICATION NUMBER (FEIN)

The Federal Employer Identification Number (FEIN) number is like a social security number for all kinds of businesses, whether for profit or nonprofit. It is a nine digit number assigned for tax filing and reporting purposes.

As confusing as it may seem – with the word *employer* in its name – you do not have to employ anyone to need this number. And to be even more confusing, it goes by other names. It is sometimes referred to as

- Employer Identification Number (EIN),
- Tax Identification Number (TIN)

The FEIN has nothing to do with designating your organization as tax exempt. Rather it identifies it as an *existing recognized business entity*. You must have an FEIN to open a bank account for your nonprofit organization, and to file your articles of organization with the state. Make sure the organization name is exactly the same with IRS as it is with the state, including any suffix (such as Inc. or Corp.) that you included in the name.

Only one FEIN is assigned to an organization and it will never expire, even if it has not been used for a long time. You cannot get a new FEIN for the same organization if you lose the number or forget it. If you have set up a bank account, you can contact the bank and retrieve the number. Or you can contact IRS by calling the Business and Specialty Tax Line at (800) 829-4933. They will give you the number over the phone if you are an authorized person (such as an officer of the organization).

THERE ARE THREE WAYS TO GET AN FEIN NUMBER:

1. Fill out and mail or fax IRS Form SS-4. You can do an internet search for the form and fill it out online, then print and mail to:

   Internal Revenue Service Center
   ATTN: EIN Operation
   Cincinnati, Ohio 45999
   You may fax the completed form to: (859) 669-5760

2. You can fill out the application online and receive the FEIN immediately if you do a search for "Apply for an Employer Identification Number (EIN) Online." You can use the number immediately, but it may take up to two weeks for IRS to get the number electronically published and working in all venues.

3. Easier yet, call IRS at (800) 829-4933 and tell them what you are starting, give them the information they request, and they will give you the FEIN over the phone and mail you confirmation in about 10 days. I recommend this method because the forms have choices for "other tax exempt organizations" that are

confusing and are not 501(c) (3) choices. Be sure to tell the IRS agent that you want to establish a 501(c) (3) organization.

There are different phone numbers for international applicants that are not toll free: (267) 941-1099 or (215) 516-6999.

NO REQUIREMENT THAT YOU *MUST* USE YOUR FEIN

Just because you get an FEIN number does not mean you have to use it, or that the IRS will be looking for a business tax return using that number. Use it when you're ready to conduct business under that number. No requirement says you must use it right away. After all, it may take a while for you to get the organization up and running.

If for some reason you change your mind or things do not work out, you need not ever use it. You are not in trouble with IRS if you get the number and never use it.

TWO WAYS TO CANCEL AN FEIN ACCOUNT:

1. If you applied with the intent to set up a nonprofit corporation and you never got around to applying for 501(c) (3) status, you can send a letter to IRS asking them to cancel the FEIN. You must tell them why, give them the FEIN number and the legal name of the organization and mailing address. Send the cancellation to:

Internal Revenue Service
Attn: EO Entity
Mail Stop 6273
Ogden, UT 84201
(Or you may fax it to (801) 620-7116).

2. If you have 501(c) (3) status and chose to terminate the organization, you must notify IRS on the appropriate annual

report, either Form 990, Form 990-N, Form 990-EZ, or Form 990-PF. They will want to know upon your dissolution or termination, if you liquidated assets as per your organizational documents.

You now have several steps out of the way. The next item on your agenda is to create a strong mission statement. More about that in the next chapter.

CHAPTER 5

DEVELOP A STRONG MISSION STATEMENT

"You can only overcome rejection when your goals are more important than approval."

—Mike Murdock

DEFINE THE MISSION YOU ARE ON

Your organization needs a mission statement. If you are the founder(s), you know better than anyone the message you want to convey about your organization. You're on a mission, and your mission statement should reflect your passion. In a sentence or two, what is that mission that motivates you? Your answer should be active, short, inspiring, and cause people to remember you. Erica Olsen states that if your mission statement would make a great T-shirt, it is probably a good one.

LEARN FROM OTHERS

To help you find the right words to express the mission for your organization, I have located a dozen of the best written U. S. nonprofit mission statements for you to study. Notice the statements that get your attention, inspire you, make you want to know more, or match your pre-existing perception of the organization.

American Diabetes Association: To prevent and cure diabetes and to improve the lives of all people affected by diabetes.

AmeriCares Foundation: In times of epic disaster or daily struggle, we deliver medical and humanitarian aid to people in need worldwide.

Feed the Children: Delivers food, medicine, clothing and other necessities to individuals, children and families who lack these essentials due to famine, war, poverty or natural disaster.

Good360: Fulfill the needs of nonprofits with corporate product donations.

Habitat For Humanity International: Seeking to put God's love into action, Habitat for Humanity brings people together to build homes, communities and hope.

Humane Society of the United States: Celebrating Animals, Confronting Cruelty.

Leukemia and Lymphoma Society: Cure leukemia, lymphoma, Hodgkin's disease and myeloma, and improve the quality of life of patients and their families.

Make a Wish Foundation of America: We grant the wishes of children with life-threatening medical conditions to enrich the human experience with hope, strength and joy.

National Multiple Sclerosis Society: We mobilize people and resources to drive research for a cure and to address the challenges of everyone affected by MS.

Smile Train: Provide a child born with a cleft the same opportunities in life as a child born without a cleft.

World Wildlife Federation: Protecting the future of nature.

Wyclilffe Bible Translators: To see a Bible translation program in progress in every language still needing one by 2025.

NOW IT'S YOUR TURN

Now it is time to develop your mission statement. Here are some guidelines to add pizzazz:

1. Keep it short: 6–15 words is normally sufficient.
2. Use active tense: Say, "Feed hungry kids!" instead of "We strive to eliminate hunger in children."
3. Try it out on others of different ages and get input.
4. Avoid jargon and formal language. Make it so clear a child could understand what is exciting about what you do. Jargon and formal language do not convey your enthusiasm. If in doubt, ask a kid.
5. Be specific about the population you serve, but do not box yourself in so that you cannot expand your reach later. Chances are you are not going to eradicate AIDS from the planet, but you can provide antiretroviral drugs to Ethiopia's poor. You may provide computers to the poor now, but what about the next latest, greatest, better-than-computers invention? You might want to say technology instead of computers so you don't limit yourself down the road.
6. Make sure your mission statement does not sound theoretical, scholarly, or academic.
7. Leave out words that water down the effectiveness of your organization. Here are a few that you should avoid:

    *   Try
    *   Attempt
    *   Aim
    *   Help

- Influence
- Endeavor
- Strive
- Pursue
- Undertake

Instead use powerful words like these:

- Prevent
- Abolish
- Confront
- Connect
- Eliminate
- Increase
- Mobilize
- Reduce
- Save
- Solve
- Transform
- Improve

8. Identify the problem you target, and the solution you provide.
9. Use clear, concise, brief, and positive terms to paint a picture of the mission you are on.

You can always change or update your mission statement later if necessary. It doesn't have to be perfect or carved in stone. For now, write it and move on. In the next chapter, you'll learn how to form your board of directors.

CHAPTER 6

FORM A BOARD OF DIRECTORS

"Opportunity is missed by most people because it is dressed in overalls and looks like work."

—Thomas Edison

NOT SHAREHOLDERS, BUT STAKEHOLDERS

Directors make up the governing body of an organization. They are not the managers; management answers to the board of directors. In profit corporations, board members are responsible to the owners, the stockholders. A nonprofit organization is not owned, so board members answer to the following:

- The public
- The government
- Their supporters
- The people the organization serves

For-profit corporations are concerned mostly about the bottom line – the money. However, in a nonprofit atmosphere, board members are not shareholders, they are *stakeholders*. They have a stake in the success of the nonprofit that has little to do with finance.

QUALIFIED AND WILLING

It is a privilege to be on a nonprofit board of directors, and members should be selected based on qualifications and willingness to serve. They do not need to have great business acumen or experience, but should have good judgment and common sense. The board should be a mix of visionaries and practical souls so that a balance exists, although harmony may not be a 24/7 accomplishment when you put dreamers and realists together. Each person should be matched to the board position that most effectively utilizes their skills and talents.

ACCOUNTANT OR ATTORNEY AS BOARD MEMBER?

There are arguments for and against having an accountant or attorney on the board. If you choose to include either, make sure your motives are not so that you can get free expertise. That is unfair to the board member and to the organization. Better to ask them for pro bono or reduced price services and select board members that have a heart for the organization's mission.

HOW MANY BOARD MEMBERS?

IRS does not specifically establish a set number of board members, but too few or too unqualified can cause delays and questions during the processing phase of your 501(c) (3) application. Relationships are also an important component of board formation. Relatives (by blood or marriage) must hold less than 50% of the vote on a board of directors. As a minimum, three board members who are not related, and if two are related, then five board members are needed to pass IRS scrutiny. There is no maximum number of board members. There should be as many as are needed to govern the organization. In addition, IRS monitors whether board members are independent members who do not benefit financially from the organization while making board decisions.

In addition to IRS codes, every state has nonprofit business statutes that spell out the minimum number of directors on the board, and the positions of those directors. Texas allows holding more than one position concurrently. Below is your statute and the board composition guidelines:

Statute: Business Organizations Code, Title 2, Corporations, Chapter 22, Nonprofit Corporations.

Minimum Board Members: 3

Required Offices: President and Secretary

*If you start with 3 members (to satisfy IRS scrutiny and state requirements), one person can be Secretary and Treasurer simultaneously.

START SMALL

To meet the requirements of IRS and the state, you need at least three board members. To start with, you might do well to keep the number of board members to a minimum. It takes less initial paperwork, fewer biographies, and fewer signatures to get everything up and running.

The fewer the board members, the less people IRS will have to scrutinize. You can add more board members after founding the organization. You might want to consider having an odd number of board members so that there is no tie when voting.

MEMBER TRAITS AND QUALITIES

Regardless of the position held by the board member, there are some defining traits and qualities that are essential to successful governance of a nonprofit organization:

- Ethical behavior and integrity
- No conflicts of interest

- Willingness to speak up and voice an opinion (even if unpopular)
- Inclination to cooperate and compromise when necessary
- Eagerness to invest the time necessary to succeed

Below are basic job descriptions for the positions on the board of directors. You can tailor the job descriptions to whatever your organization needs from the board members. You can call the positions whatever you want, you are not limited to the titles given.

President (or Chairman) of the Board

Chairman sounds more like a title for a profit corporation, so President is often used for nonprofit corporations. Helpful attributes include:

- Leadership skills
- Earned respect of board members
- Good communication skills
- Ability to make hard calls when difficult decisions must be made
- Willingness to delegate

If you are the founder and you have those qualifications, then consider making yourself the initial President of the Board of Directors. You may be the most qualified person for the job.

A sample job description might be:

> *The President of the Board represents the organization as ambassador to the community; presides over the affairs of the board and assists in setting agendas for board meetings; coordinates establishment of committees, assignments, and execution of tasks; steers board selection of an Executive Director; leads strategic planning and fundraising efforts; recruits and trains new board members; and delegates responsibility and authority to accomplish the goals of the organization.*

Vice President (or Vice Chairman) of the Board

The Vice President is sometimes the successor to the President, a President in Training, or President-elect. The corporate bylaws should reflect whether that is the case. Helpful attributes for Vice President are the same as for the President.

A sample job description might be:

> *The Vice President of the Board acts as the President when the President is not available. He or she assists the President in executing duties, and performs other duties as assigned by the Board.*

Secretary of the Board

The Secretary of the Board is the communication and recordkeeping member of the Board of Directors. He or she should be familiar with the mission and vision of the organization, the Certificate of Formation, and the bylaws. Helpful attributes include an aptitude for organization, writing abilities, and communication competence.

A sample job description might be:

> *The Secretary of the Board maintains records of all Board actions; prepares and distributes meeting minutes; safeguards all corporation records; presides over meetings in the absence of the President and Vice President; and performs other duties as assigned by the Board.*

Treasurer (or Chief Financial Officer, CFO)

The Treasurer or CFO is the go-to person for financial questions in an organization. He or she must be above reproach in integrity, and maintain transparency in performing the duties of the office. Helpful attributes for Treasurer include critical thinking skills, analytical ability, and willingness to learn financial accounting principles as they relate to nonprofit organizations.

A sample job description might be:

> *The Treasurer coordinates and ensures financial stewardship and financial wellbeing of the organization; manages finances; ensures timely and accurate filing of financial reports to IRS and state agencies; presents annual budgets for board approval; reviews annual audits; signs and deposits checks; and performs other duties as assigned by the Board.*

Board Member or Organizational Director

Not every member of the Board of Directors needs to hold a title to an office. All positions are important and add to the effective governance of a nonprofit organization. Each board member should be a volunteer who is committed to the mission of the organization. This is a person who is willing to make time and actively participate in board meetings, fundraising activities, and public events involving the organization. In addition to investing time, board members should also be willing to invest money. Each member should have a copy of the organization's conflict of interest policy, and sign a disclosure form annually.

A sample job description might be:

> *Board Members attend regularly scheduled board meetings; actively participate in decision making, considering the best interest of the organization; maintain integrity in use of resources; adhere to the letter and intent of regulatory guidance; establish and carry out planning, policies, fundraising, and budgeting; and evaluate the Executive Director's (if there is one) performance and compensation annually.*

With your board of directors now in place, you are ready to create your IRS-Compliant Organizing Document. Don't get nervous. You'll see that it's not at all difficult!

CHAPTER 7

PREPARE IRS-COMPLIANT ORGANIZING DOCUMENT

"Nothing will ever be attempted, if all possible objections must first be overcome."

—Samuel Jackson

THE BIRTH OF AN ORGANIZATION

When a child is born, a vital record of that birth is created in the state in which the child was born – it's called the Birth Certificate. It's recorded by the state and it registers the presence of a new little person. The certificate documents who the parents are, where and when the child was born, and other important information verifying the child's existence. The child is given a name, and in some cases, a suffix (such as Jr. or III) that further identifies the child. The child's origin is declared, such as Caucasian, Hispanic, or Native American. You complete the paperwork and it is send to the bureau of vital records and a birth certificate is created.

When a nonprofit corporation is born, a vital record of that birth is created in the state in which the organization was born – it's normally called the Articles of Incorporation, but in Texas, the same document is called Certificate of Formation. It is recorded by the state and it registers the presence of a new organization. This declares who the parents are, where and when the organization was born, and other vital information verifying the organization's existence. The nonprofit is given a name, and in some cases, a suffix (such as Inc. or Corp.) that further identifies the organization. The nonprofit's origin is declared, such as Public Benefit, Mutual Benefit, or Religious. You complete the paperwork and send it in to the Secretary of State and a *business birth certificate* (figuratively speaking) is created.

A MATTER OF PUBLIC RECORD

A birth certificate is a public record in the sense that if you are related and have a need to know, you can get a copy of a birth certificate. The analogy differs when compared to a nonprofit corporation. Certificates of Formation are public records and as such are available to the public. Anyone wishing access is allowed to see, read, and have a copy of your nonprofit's birth certificate. For this reason, it's a good idea to leave out social security numbers and other personal identifiers in the documents you file.

Public charitable foundations, funds, community chests, and some trusts may also be eligible for 501(c) (3) status under certain circumstances, as long as they exist for charitable purposes. Their filing requirements are similar to nonprofit corporations, but their documents have different names, such as Articles of Association instead of Certificates of Formation. Incorporation provides more legal protection for officers than unincorporated organizations.

TYPES OF NONPROFITS

To establish this vital record with your Secretary of State and IRS, you must decide the origin or type of organization because it has far-reaching consequences for 501(c) (3) status. There are three basic origins or types of nonprofits:

Public Benefit

This is normally a charity with a charitable mission, and IRS recognizes this type of organization for 501(c) (3) status. A public benefit corporation cannot be established to help just one organization (such as a particular orphanage) or individual (such as a particular orphan), but must benefit a class of people or group of organizations (such as potentially benefiting any orphan or orphanage in Mexico). You can start small by actually benefiting one or two particular orphanages, but must allow for helping others in the same category or class. If it benefits only one organization or a defined finite group of people who can be identified by name, such as a family, it is a private foundation, not a nonprofit corporation. This does not mean you cannot help an individual or a family, but that you cannot limit your efforts in establishing a nonprofit to specific people or families, you must leave room to grow and add people or families whose names you do not know yet, and who you do not even know need your help right now.

Public benefit organizations handling less than $5,000 per year are automatically exempt and do not need to file for 501(c) (3) status unless they want contributions to be deductible.

The Frisco Ballet is an example of a Public Benefit nonprofit.

Mutual Benefit

This type of nonprofit benefits members of a group. It is similar to a club. People pay membership fees or join the group, and assets are distributed among the members if the organization dissolves. IRS does not normally give 501(c) (3) status to mutual benefit organizations because they serve their members, not the public. An example is the Dixie Volunteer Fire Department in Tyler, a nonprofit, but not a 501(c) (3) tax exempt nonprofit.

Religious

This type of nonprofit is eligible for 501(c) (3) status and can be a church, or it can be a religious organization established to study or advance religion. It if is a church, it has no requirement to file annual reports declaring income and expenses like other 501(c) (3) organizations must do. There are several requirements for churches that want 501(c) (3) status. They must have a doctrine of beliefs, scheduled services, and a stable congregation, among other requirements. Churches do not have to apply for 501(c) (3) status, but many do because their supporters are assured that contributions are tax deductible.

Lakewood Church in Houston is an example of a religious 501(c) (3).

FOREIGN VS. DOMESTIC CORPORATION

To conduct nonprofit business in other states, you must first be recognized as a nonprofit entity in your own state by filing origination documents such as *Articles of Incorporation*, which gets you a business birth certificate, figuratively speaking. Then you can apply to the Secretary of State in other states as a *foreign* nonprofit corporation for recognition and approval to conduct nonprofit business in their state. *Foreign* does not mean foreign country, it means from outside the state boundaries, thus not an in-state or *domestic* organization. It normally costs more to be registered as a foreign nonprofit corporation than a domestic nonprofit in a state. Outsiders usually get charged more.

The way to get recognized is by filling out an application for authorization from the other state or states. This approval is normally given for a fee, and is usually called a *Certificate of Authority*. Each state has its own requirements, fees, and forms. Most states require some kind of proof that you are approved and your organization is doing reputable business in your home state. This requirement is usually met by providing a recently certified copy of your state's Certificate of Good Standing, Certificate of Existence, Certificate of Fact (Texas), or similar state document. It is a piece of paper provided by your Secretary of State that you pay to have certified, usually not more than 60 days prior to applying to another state for approval to conduct business. If it gets too old, you have to pay to get another copy certified.

REQUIREMENT FOR REGISTERED AGENT

To do business as either a domestic or a foreign nonprofit corporation, you must have a *registered agent*. This is a person or business in the state that you want to conduct the affairs of your nonprofit. The agent's purpose is to give the Secretary of State a contact person with a street address (as opposed to a post office box) inside state lines who will receive official mail, handle complaints, answer telephone inquiries if they need to call about something, and just generally be the go-to person or company on behalf of your nonprofit.

Your nonprofit cannot be its own registered agent, but you can be a registered agent for your organization in your state if you are willing to be the face and voice behind the corporate name and mission. The registered agent can be a commercial or noncommercial agent. It can be an individual or organization willing to be your representative, or it can be a company for hire who is licensed by the state to represent other organizations.

To find a commercial registered agent, you can do an internet search for registered agent and the state, or you can call the Secretary of State's office and ask for a list of approved registered agents in the state.

REQUIRED STATEMENTS FOR IRS 501(C) (3) APPROVAL

The exact wording of your Certificate of Formation or similar document is not critical except for a few required statements that if missing, will cause your application for 501(c) (3) status to be rejected. If IRS *suggests* something, it is a good idea to follow the suggestion. Here is the IRS *suggested* wording to meet their required language and statements:

Benefit Statement:

No part of the net earnings of the corporation shall inure to the benefit, or be distributable to its members, trustees, officers, or other private persons, except that the corporation shall be authorized and empowered to pay reasonable compensation for services rendered and to make payments and distributions in furtherance of the purposes set forth in previous articles hereof. No substantial part of the activities of the corporation shall be the carrying on of propaganda, or otherwise attempting to influence legislation, and the corporation shall not participate in, or intervene in (including the publishing or distribution of statements) any political campaign on behalf or in opposition to any candidate for public office. Notwithstanding any other provision of these articles, the corporation shall not carry on any other activities not permitted to be carried on (a) by a corporation exempt from federal income tax under Section 501(c) (3) of the Internal Revenue Code, or the corresponding section of any future federal tax code, or (b) by a corporation, contributions to which are deductible under Section 170(c) (2) of the Internal Revenue Code, or the corresponding section of any future federal tax code.

Purpose Statement:

Said Corporation is organized exclusively for charitable, religious, educational, and scientific purposes, including, for such purposes, the making of distributions to organizations that qualify as exempt organizations under Section 501(c) (3) of the Internal Revenue Code, or the corresponding section of any future federal tax code.

Dissolution Statement:

Upon the dissolution of the corporation, assets shall be distributed for one or more exempt purposes within the meaning of Section 501(c) (3) of the Internal Revenue Code, or corresponding section of any future federal tax code, or shall be distributed to the federal government, or to a state or local government, for a public purpose. Any such assets not so disposed of shall be disposed of by a Court of Competent Jurisdiction of the county in which the principal office of the corporation is then located, exclusively for such purposes or to such organization or organizations as said Court shall determine which are organized and operated exclusively for such purposes.

Now that you know and understand the concept of the Certificate of Formation, in the next chapter we'll take a look at what should be included in that document.

CHAPTER 8

WHAT TO INCLUDE IN CERTIFICATE OF FORMATION

"The best time to start building the castle of your dreams is always going to be right now."

—Gonzo Arzuag

INFORMATION FOR CERTIFICATE OF FORMATION

There is some relatively constant information across states that must be included in the Certificate of Formation. Virtually every state requires the following:

- Name of the corporation
- Type of corporation: public benefit, mutual benefit, or religious
- Duration (normally perpetual)
- Street address and mailing address of the initial registered office and the name of the initial registered agent
- The name of the incorporator(s)
- The required IRS purpose, benefit, and dissolution clauses (see previous chapter)
- Whether the corporation has members (most nonprofits DO NOT have members).

- Who will manage the affairs of the corporation (normally the Board of Directors)
- The number of directors (make sure you include the required positions for your state)
- The term and manner of election of directors (you can say that they will be as provided or described in the Bylaws)
- A statement that the corporation shall have all powers given to a nonprofit corporation as per Business Organizations Code, Title 2, Corporations, Chapter 22, Nonprofit Corporations, and an exempt organization as described in Section 501(c) (3) of the Internal Revenue Code of 1986, as amended (or the corresponding provision of any future laws of the State of Texas and Internal Revenue Law).
- That the Articles can be amended by the Board of Directors in the manner provided by the Bylaws (unless you want to include those details in the incorporation documents)
- Articles to protect directors and officers from lawsuits
- A statement that the corporation may purchase general comprehensive liability insurance covering the board members and officers in the performance of their duties
- An affirmation that all information is true and correct, and execution by signature(s) by the incorporator(s) on a specific date

Following is a Certificate of Formation template prepared by an attorney so that you do not have to prepare one from scratch.

NOTE: If you do not want to go to the trouble of writing or typing out the Certificate of Formation, you can go to www.doyourownnonprofit.com and purchase the template for a small fee. All you have to do is fill in the blanks with your organization's information, print and file. Saves lots of work and has legal integrity (nothing important is missing for the state or IRS).

CERTIFICATE OF FORMATION OF NON-PROFIT CORPORATION
(DOMESTIC – TEXAS)

ARTICLE I

NAME

1.01 Name

The legal name of this corporation shall be [insert legal name of corporation). The business of the corporation may be conducted as [name of corporation and/or registered fictitious business name(s) or so-called dba(s), if any].

ARTICLE II

DURATION

2.01 Duration

The period of duration of the corporation shall be perpetual.

ARTICLE III

PURPOSE

3.01 Purpose

[Legal name of the corporation] is a non-profit corporation organized exclusively for charitable, religious, educational, and scientific purposes, including, for such purposes, the making of distributions to organizations that qualify as exempt organizations, under Section 501 (c)(3) of the Internal Revenue Code, or the corresponding section of any future federal tax code.

[Optional – Detailed statement of purpose. Here's an example: We provide education by giving free music lessons and instruments to underprivileged children in the United States and all over the world. We send out talented ambassador musicians to teach children music awareness, how to play instruments of all kinds, and how to write and perform songs of all genres. To maximize our effectiveness, we may seek to collaborate with other non-profit organizations which qualify as non-profit corporations under Section 501(c)(3).]

3.02 Public Benefit

[Legal name of the corporation] is designated as a public benefit corporation.

ARTICLE IV

NON-PROFIT NATURE / BENEFITS

4.01 Non-profit Nature

[Legal name of the corporation] is not organized and shall not be operated for the private gain of any person. The property of the corporation is irrevocably dedicated to its charitable, religious, educational or scientific purposes. No part of the assets, receipts, or net earnings of the corporation shall inure to the benefit of, or be distributed to, any individual. The corporation may, however, pay reasonable compensation for services rendered, and make other payments and distributions consistent with these Articles.

4.02 Personal Liability

No officer or director of this corporation shall be personally liable for the debts or obligations of [legal name of corporation] of any nature whatsoever, nor shall any of the property or assets of the officers or directors be subject to the payment of the debts or obligations of this corporation.

4.03 Dissolution

Upon termination or dissolution of the [legal name of corporation], any assets lawfully available for distribution shall be distributed to one or more qualifying organizations described in Section 501(c)(3) of the Internal Revenue Code of 1986 (or described in any corresponding provision of any successor statute), which organization or organizations shall have a charitable purpose which, at least generally, includes a purpose similar to the terminating or dissolving corporation.

The organization to receive the assets of the [legal name of corporation] hereunder shall be selected by the discretion of a majority of the managing body of the [legal name of corporation] and if its members cannot so agree, then the recipient organization shall be selected pursuant to a verified petition in equity filed in a court of proper jurisdiction against the [legal name of corporation] by one or more of its managing body, which verified petition shall contain such statements as reasonably indicate the applicability of this section. The court upon a finding that this section is applicable shall select the qualifying organization or organizations to receive the assets to be distributed, giving preference if practicable to organizations located within Texas.

In the event the court shall find that this section is applicable but that there is no qualifying organization known to it which has a charitable purpose which, at least generally, includes a purpose similar to this corporation, then the court shall direct the distribution of its assets lawfully available for distribution to the Treasurer of the State of Texas to be added to the general fund.

4.04 Prohibited Distributions

No part of the net earnings, or properties of this corporation, on dissolution or otherwise, shall inure to the benefit of, or be distributable to, its members, directors, officers or other private person or individual, except that the corporation shall be authorized and empowered to pay reasonable compensation for services rendered and to make payments and distributions in furtherance of the purposes set forth in Article III, Section 3.01.

4.05 Restricted Activities

No substantial part of the corporation's activities shall be the carrying on of propaganda, or otherwise attempting to influence legislation, and the corporation shall not participate in, or intervene (including the publishing or distribution of statements) in any political campaign on behalf of or in opposition to any candidate for public office.

4.06 Prohibited Activities

Notwithstanding any other provision of these Articles, the corporation shall not carry on any activities not permitted to be carried on (a) by a corporation exempt from federal income tax as an organization described by Section 501(c)(3) of the Internal Revenue Code, or the corresponding section of any future federal tax code, or (b) by a corporation, contributions to which are deductible under Section 170(c)(2) of the Internal Revenue Code, or the corresponding section of any future federal tax code.

ARTICLE V

BOARD OF DIRECTORS

5.01 Governance

[Legal name of the corporation] shall be governed by its board of directors.

5.02 Initial Directors

The initial directors of the corporation shall be [insert names of directors here].

ARTICLE VI

MEMBERSHIP

6.01 Membership

[Legal name of the corporation] shall have no members. The management of the affairs of the corporation shall be vested in a board of directors, as defined in the corporation's bylaws.

ARTICLE VII

AMENDMENTS

7.01 Amendments

Any amendment to the Certificate of Formation may be adopted by approval of two-thirds (2/3) of the board of directors.

ARTICLE VIII

ADDRESSES OF THE CORPORATION

8.01 Corporate Address

The physical address of the corporation is: [insert corporate address here].

The mailing address of the corporation is: [insert corporate mailing address here].

ARTICLE IX

APPOINTMENT OF REGISTERED AGENT

9.01 Registered Agent

The registered agent of the corporation shall be: [insert name and address of registered agent here].

ARTICLE X

INCORPORATOR

The incorporators of the corporation are as follow:

[Insert name(s) of incorporator(s) and their respective addresses here].

CERTIFICATE OF ADOPTION OF CERTIFICATE OF FORMATION

We, the undersigned, do hereby certify that the above-stated Certificate of Formation of [legal name of corporation] were approved by the Board of Directors on [insert exact date] and constitute a complete copy of Certificate of Formation of the [legal name of corporation].

[List names, addresses and signatures of all directors and incorporators.]

_____Address: _____

By: _____Date: _____

_____Address: _____

By: _____Date: _____

_____Address: _____

By: _____Date: _____

Acknowledgment of consent to appointment as registered agent:

I, [name of registered agent], agree to be the registered agent for [legal name of corporation] as appointed herein.

Registered Agent

_____Address: _____

By: _____Date: _____

CHAPTER 9

STATE GUIDELINES FOR NONPROFIT CORPORATIONS

"As long as you're going to be thinking anyway, think big."
—Donald Trump

GUIDELINES FOR TEXAS FILING

Domestic corporations file Certificate of Formation.

Foreign corporations file Application for Registration.

Certificate of Formation for a Nonprofit Corporation (Form 202) is available at http://www.sos.state.tx.us but does not include IRS 501(c) (3) required language. You can add it in the blanks provided or submit your own document.

Nonprofit Corporation Application for Registration (Form 302) is available at http://www.sos.state.tx.us

Filing fee is $25.00 (domestic or foreign) payable to Secretary of State. Expedite fee is $25.00.

Send original and copy of documents to:

> Secretary of State
> PO Box 13697
> Austin, TX 78711-3697

Forms can be faxed to (512) 463-5709 along with Form 807, available at https://webservices.sos.state.tx.us/forms/payment.pdf

Forms can be delivered to:

> James Earl Rudder Office Building
> 1019 Brazos
> Austin, TX 78701

For questions, call (512) 463-5555.

CHAPTER 10

WHAT TO INCLUDE IN ORGANIZATIONAL BYLAWS

"A goal is a dream with a deadline."

—Napoleon Hill

WHAT ARE THE STANDARD OPERATING PROCEDURES?

Have you ever been around someone who was or is in the military? They have a language all their own. One of the things they often say is, "It's SOP." What they mean is it's *standard operating procedure.* In my ten years in the United States Air Force, there were SOPs for everything, normally in the form of regulations, manuals, and technical orders. There was written guidance that addressed just about every foreseeable event or circumstance.

If you look at the nonprofit you are creating as its own army to do good things in the world, you will see the need for SOPs to make your operation as efficient as an Army or Marine rifle platoon. Because you are the incorporator, you may be filling the shoes right now of the Platoon Leader (President), Platoon Sergeant (Vice President), Company Clerk (Secretary), or Quartermaster (Treasurer). People have to know the rules and what is expected so that they can follow them. Your nonprofit corporation bylaws establish the rules or SOPs in which business is conducted.

CREATING THE CONSTITUTION

Another way to understand the significance of bylaws is to think of them as the organization's constitution. You cannot put everything in the Constitution, only the really important stuff. A good rule of thumb is to put as little in the bylaws as possible. Once it is written and approved, it's the way things are done. If you ever want to change something, you have to amend the bylaws, just as you would have to amend the Constitution. Keep trivial aspects that are subject to change (such as the day of the week board meetings are held) out of the bylaws. Be sure to attach any changes to the bylaws directly to the master copy as soon as changes are made.

It is not uncommon to make a change, put it in the meeting minutes, but then forget which meeting the change was made, and it is never attached to the master copy of the bylaws. The solution is to assign the responsibility to update the bylaws to one of the board positions. If you keep it simple, there will not be many changes to keep up with.

BYLAW CONTENTS

So exactly what do you put in the bylaws? It depends on which state you live in, but there are some general items addressed in virtually all nonprofit bylaws:

1. Name of the organization and the mission.
2. How many board members (minimum established by the state) and what constitutes a quorum? (Normally a majority of members be present.)
3. Qualifications of board members.
4. How officers and board members will be elected or appointed and how long they will serve. If you want them to be able to serve more than one term, you need to say so in the bylaws. Also address limitations on personal liability. What are the procedures for removing a board member if necessary?

5. Duties of Board Members

6. Procedures for calling and conducting meetings, including special and emergency board meetings; and when regular meetings will be held (suggest monthly, bi-monthly, or quarterly, nothing more specific so that you have flexibility to make changes).

   In this era of electronics, will you allow board meetings by email, teleconferencing, and/or electronic conferencing software such as Skype? Each state has its own laws about what is acceptable, and not all states have caught up to technology. Texas statutes neither allow nor disallow or disallow use of teleconferencing for meetings. You address it in your bylaws. Most states allow members to use teleconferencing and be counted present as long everyone can simultaneously hear each other during the meeting.

7. How will conflicts of interest be handled? I suggest you reference a conflict of interest policy so that if you ever change procedures, you can more easily update a conflict of interest policy than make formal changes to bylaws.

8. How funds will be accounted for and disbursed.

9. If the nonprofit has members, what are the rights of membership? (Most 501(c) (3) nonprofits do not have members).

10. How committees can be convened and dissolved.

11. How can bylaws be changed (for example, by majority vote of the board)?

12. Choose an accounting or fiscal year. This should fit with the normal flow of activities. Education related activities might need a different fiscal year than an animal shelter.

13. Authorize bank signatories.

The following pages include a template for Texas nonprofit bylaws drawn up by an attorney so that you know it contains legal integrity and everything you need to be compliant with the state and IRS. You can delete or modify anything that does not apply to your organization or anything you would rather do differently, but you might be hard pressed to find anything to add. The attorney who created this document was very thorough.

Here are a few things to be aware of in this template:

1. 2.03 Nonprofit Status and Exempt Activities Limitation. This section says that you are already approved for 501(c) (3) status. I have it from the attorney's lips that "It is standard practice" to include this clause now so that you do not have to amend the Bylaws later. (per Steve Eggleston, J.D.)

2. 4.01 Number of Directors. The template is set up with a minimum of 4 directors to cover the four main positions of President, Vice President, Secretary, and Treasurer. Texas requires three board members minimum, and you can combine the positions of Secretary and Treasurer if you choose, but President and Secretary must be two separate people.

3. 4.08 Manner of Acting. Paragraph (d) allows meetings to take place by means of modern technology so everyone does not have to be physically present to be considered in attendance. The entire meeting can be by telephone!

4. 5.3 Informal Action By The Board of Directors. This section gives the Board the right to give consent without a meeting, allowing email to be used when a meeting is not needed.

5. 6.05 Vice President. The Vice President moves up to President at the end of the President's term. You can change this provision if you do not want it to work that way in your organization.

6. 8.02 Fiscal Year. The fiscal year is January 1 – December 31. You can change the date if your organization needs a different fiscal year.

7. 11.03 Means and Conditions of Disclosure. Nonprofits have a lawful obligation to disclose certain documents. This section should be reviewed to make sure that the procedures for disclosure (via the organization's website) is the way you

want to handle disclosure. It is the easiest and eliminates all individual inquiries to see your documents, and thus reduces administrative workload. You decide and change the wording to suit your organization.

If you do not want to go to the trouble of writing bylaws from scratch or typing out the following pages, you can go to www. doyourownnonprofit.com and purchase the template for Texas nonprofit bylaws for a small fee. All you have to do is fill in the blanks (actually brackets with instructions) with your organization's information and print.

NON-PROFIT CORPORATE BYLAWS

(TEXAS)

ARTICLE I

NAME

1.01 Name

The name of this corporation shall be [insert the legal name of your non-profit and any other legal name under which it may be conducted].

[Example: The name of this corporation shall be Transcontinental Humanitarian Corp. The business of the corporation may be conducted as Transcontinental Humanitarian Corp. or Transcontinental Humanitarian Expedition.]

ARTICLE II

PURPOSES AND POWERS

2.01 Purpose

[Insert the legal name of your non-profit – hereafter referred to as "The Corporation"] is a non-profit corporation and shall be operated exclusively for charitable, religious, educational, and scientific purposes, including, for such purposes, the making of distributions to organizations that qualify as exempt organizations, under Section 501 (c)(3) of the Internal Revenue Code, or the corresponding section of any future federal tax code.

[The Corporation]'s purpose is to [insert description of specific purpose].

[Example: Transcontinental Humanitarian Corp. is a non-profit corporation and shall be operated exclusively for educational and charitable purposes within the meaning of Section 501 (c)(3) of the Internal Revenue Code of 1986, or the corresponding section of any future Federal tax code.

Transcontinental Humanitarian Corp.'s purpose is to address, educate, coordinate, and provide aid and relief to eradicate chronic malnutrition and hunger on a local and global level.

We provide education by giving free lectures and slideshows titled "The World Hunger Exhibition," in schools, libraries, and other public venues as well as utilizing social media channels and the corporation's website to provide facts, statistics, and other related data on causes, current efforts and solutions to eradicating chronic malnutrition and hunger.

Our programs include sending out ambassadors to raise social consciousness about the cause on a local and global level, and to hold fundraising events in order to provide immediate relief and assistance to those suffering from chronic malnutrition and hunger regardless of their race, ethnicity, or religion.

To maximize our impact on current efforts, we may seek to collaborate with other non-profit organizations which fall under the 501(c) (3) Section of the Internal Revenue Code and are operated exclusively for educational and charitable purposes.

At times, per the discretion of the Board of Directors, we may provide internships or volunteer opportunities which shall provide opportunities for involvement in said activities and programs in order to have a greater impact for change.]

2.02 Powers

The corporation shall have the power, directly or indirectly, alone or in conjunction or cooperation with others, to do any and all lawful acts which may be necessary or convenient to affect the charitable purposes, for which the corporation is organized, and to aid or assist other organizations or persons whose activities further accomplish, foster, or attain such purposes. The powers of the corporation may include, but not be limited to, the acceptance of contributions from the public and private sectors, whether financial or in-kind contributions.

2.03 Nonprofit Status and Exempt Activities Limitation.

a. Nonprofit Legal Status. [The Corporation] is a Texas non-profit public benefit corporation, recognized as tax exempt under Section 501(c)(3) of the United States Internal Revenue Code.

b. Exempt Activities Limitation. Notwithstanding any other provision of these Bylaws, no Director, officer, employee, member, or representative of this corporation shall take any action or carry on any activity by or on behalf of the corporation not permitted to be taken or carried on by an organization exempt under Section 501(c)(3) of the Internal Revenue Code as it now exists or may be amended, or by any organization contributions to which are deductible under Section 170(c)(2) of such Code and Regulations as it now exists or may be amended. No part of the net earnings of the corporation shall inure to the benefit or be distributable to any Director, officer, member, or other private person, except that the corporation shall be authorized and empowered to pay reasonable compensation for services rendered and to make payments and distributions in furtherance of the purposes set forth in the Certificate of Formation and these Bylaws.

c. Distribution Upon Dissolution. Upon termination or dissolution of [the Corporation], any assets lawfully available for distribution shall be distributed to one (1) or more qualifying organizations described in Section 501(c)(3) of the 1986 Internal Revenue Code (or described in any corresponding provision of any successor statute) which organization or organizations have a charitable purpose which, at least generally, includes a purpose similar to the terminating or dissolving corporation.

The organization to receive the assets of [the Corporation] hereunder shall be selected in the discretion of a majority of the managing body of the corporation, and if its members cannot so agree, then the recipient organization shall be selected pursuant to a Verified Petition in equity, or such other court of appropriate jurisdiction, filed in a court of proper jurisdiction against [the Corporation], by one (1) or more of its managing body, which Verified Petition shall contain such statements as reasonably indicate the applicability of this section. The court upon a finding that this section is applicable shall select the qualifying organization or organizations to receive the assets to be distributed, giving preference if practicable to organizations located within the State of Texas.

In the event that the court shall find that this section is applicable but that there is no qualifying organization known to it which has a charitable purpose, which, at least generally, includes a purpose similar to [the Corporation], then the court shall direct the distribution of its assets lawfully available for distribution to the Treasurer of the State of Texas to be added to the general fund.

ARTICLE III

MEMBERSHIP

3.01 No Membership Classes

The corporation shall have no members who have any right to vote or title or interest in or to the corporation, its properties and franchises.

3.02 Non-Voting Affiliates

The Board of Directors may approve classes of non-voting affiliates with rights, privileges, and obligations established by the Board. Affiliates may be individuals, businesses, and other organizations that seek to support the mission of the corporation. The Board, a designated committee of the Board, or any duly-elected officer in accordance with Board policy, shall have authority to admit any individual or organization as an affiliate, to recognize representatives of affiliates, and to make determinations as to affiliates' rights, privileges, and obligations. At no time shall affiliate information be shared with or sold to other organizations or groups without the affiliate's consent. At the discretion of the Board of Directors, affiliates may be given endorsement, recognition and media coverage at fundraising activities, clinics, other events or at the corporation website. Affiliates have no voting rights, and are not members of the corporation.

3.03 Dues

Any dues for affiliates shall be determined by the Board of Directors.

ARTICLE IV

BOARD OF DIRECTORS

4.01 Number of Directors

[The Corporation] shall have a Board of Directors consisting of at least 4 and no more than 15 Directors. Within these limits, the Board may increase or decrease the number of Directors serving on the Board, including for the purpose of staggering the terms of Directors.

4.02 Powers

All corporate powers shall be exercised by or under the authority of the Board and the affairs of [the Corporation] shall be managed under the direction of the Board, except as otherwise provided by law.

4.03 Terms

   a.   All Directors shall be elected to serve a one-year term; however, the term may be extended until a successor has been elected.
   b.   Director terms shall be staggered so that approximately half the number of Directors will end their terms in any given year.
   c.   Directors may serve terms in succession.
   d.   The term of office shall be considered to begin January 1 and end December 31 of the second year in office, unless the term is extended until such time as a successor has been elected.

4.04 Qualifications and Election of Directors

In order to be eligible to serve as a Director on the Board of Directors, the individual must be 18 years of age and an affiliate within affiliate classifications created by the Board of Directors. Directors may be elected at any Board meeting by the majority vote of the existing Board of Directors. The election of Directors to replace those who have fulfilled their term of office shall take place in January of each year.

4.05 Vacancies

The Board of Directors may fill vacancies due to the expiration of a Director's term of office, resignation, death, or removal of a Director or may appoint new Directors to fill a previously unfilled Board position, subject to the maximum number of Directors under these Bylaws.

(a) Unexpected Vacancies. Vacancies in the Board of Directors due to resignation, death, or removal shall be filled by the Board for the balance of the term of the Director being replaced.

4.06 Removal of Directors

A Director may be removed by [insert your choice between "a majority or "two-thirds"] vote of the Board of Directors then in office, if:

a. the Director is absent and unexcused from two or more meetings of the Board of Directors in a twelve-month period. The Board President is empowered to excuse Directors from attendance for a reason deemed adequate by the Board President. The President shall not have the power to excuse him/herself from the Board meeting attendance, and in that case, the Board Vice President shall excuse the President. Or:

b. for cause or no cause, if before any meeting of the Board at which a vote on removal will be made the Director in question is given electronic or written notification of the Board's intention to discuss her/his case and is given the opportunity to be heard at a meeting of the Board.

4.07 Board of Directors Meetings

a. Regular Meetings. The Board of Directors shall have a minimum of four (4) regular meetings each calendar year at times and places fixed by the Board. Board meetings shall be held upon four (4) days notice by first-class mail, electronic mail, or facsimile transmission or forty-eight (48) hours notice delivered personally or by telephone. If sent by mail, facsimile transmission, or electronic mail, the notice shall be deemed to be delivered upon its deposit in the mail or transmission system. Notice of meetings shall specify the place, day, and hour of meeting. The purpose of the meeting need not be specified.

b. Special Meetings. Special meetings of the Board may be called by the President, Vice President, Secretary, Treasurer, or any two (2) other Directors of the Board of Directors. A special meeting must be preceded by at least 2-days notice to each Director of the date, time, and place, but not the purpose, of the meeting.

c. Waiver of Notice. Any Director may waive notice of any meeting, in accordance with Texas statutes.

4.08 Manner of Acting.

a. Quorum. A majority of the Directors in office immediately before a meeting shall constitute a quorum for the transaction of business at that meeting of the Board. No business shall be considered by the Board at any meeting at which a quorum is not present.

b. Majority Vote. Except as otherwise required by law or by the Certificate of Formation, the act of the majority of the Directors present at a meeting at which a quorum is present shall be the act of the Board.

c. Hung Board Decisions. On the occasion that Directors of the Board are unable to make a decision based on a tied number of votes, the President or Treasurer in the order of presence shall have the power to swing the vote based on his/her discretion.

d. Participation. Except as required otherwise by law, the Certificate of Formation, or these Bylaws, Directors may participate in a regular or special meeting through the use of any means of communication by which all Directors participating may simultaneously hear each other during the meeting, including in person, internet video meeting or by telephonic conference call.

4.09 Compensation for Board Service

Directors [insert your choice on whether your Board members "shall receive the following compensation _____" or "shall receive no compensation"] for carrying out their duties as Directors. The Board may adopt policies providing for reasonable reimbursement of Directors for expenses incurred in conjunction with carrying out Board responsibilities, such as travel expenses to attend Board meetings.

4.10 Compensation for Professional Services by Directors

Directors are not restricted from being remunerated for professional services provided to the corporation. Such remuneration shall be reasonable and fair to the corporation and must be reviewed and approved in accordance with the Board Conflict of Interest policy and applicable state law or law of the U.S. territory.

ARTICLE V

COMMITTEES

5.01 Committees

The Board of Directors may, by the resolution adopted by a majority of the Directors then in office, designate one or more committees, each consisting of two or more Directors, to serve at the pleasure of the Board. Any committee, to the extent provided in the resolution of the Board, shall have all the authority of the Board, except that no committee, regardless of Board resolution, may:

a. take any final action on matters which also requires Board members' approval or approval of a majority of all members;
b. fill vacancies on the Board of Directors or in any committee which has the authority of the Board;

c. amend or repeal Bylaws or adopt new Bylaws;

d. amend or repeal any resolution of the Board of Directors which by its express terms is not so amendable or repealable;

e. appoint any other committees of the Board of Directors or the members of these committees;

f. expend corporate funds to support a nominee for Director; or

g. approve any transaction;

i. to which the corporation is a party and one or more Directors have a material financial interest; or

ii. between the corporation and one or more of its Directors or between the corporation or any person in which one or more of its Directors have a material financial interest.

5.2 Meetings and Action of Committees

Meetings and action of the committees shall be governed by, and held and taken in accordance with, the provisions of Article IV of these Bylaws concerning meetings of the Directors, with such changes in the context of those Bylaws as are necessary to substitute the committee and its members for the Board of Directors and its members, except that the time for regular meetings of committees may be determined either by resolution of the Board of Directors or by resolution of the committee. Special meetings of the committee may also be called by resolution of the Board of Directors. Notice of special meetings of committees shall also be given to any and all alternate members, who shall have the right to attend all meetings of the committee. Minutes shall be kept of each meeting of any committee and shall be filed with the corporate records. The Board of Directors may adopt rules for the governing of the committee not inconsistent with the provision of these Bylaws.

5.3 Informal Action By The Board of Directors

Any action required or permitted to be taken by the Board of Directors at a meeting may be taken without a meeting if consent in writing, setting forth the action so taken, shall be agreed by the consensus of a quorum. For purposes of this section, an e-mail transmission from an e-mail address on record constitutes a valid writing. The intent of this provision is to allow the Board of Directors to use email to approve actions, as long as a quorum of Board members gives consent.

ARTICLE VI

OFFICERS

6.01 Board Officers

The officers of the corporation shall be a Board President, Vice President, Secretary, and Treasurer, all of whom shall be chosen by, and serve at the pleasure of, the Board of Directors. Each Board officer shall have the authority and shall perform the duties set forth in these Bylaws or by resolution of the Board or by direction of an officer authorized by the Board to prescribe the duties and authority of other officers. The Board may also appoint additional Vice Presidents and such other officers as it deems expedient for the proper conduct of the business of the corporation, each of whom shall have such authority and shall perform such duties as the Board of Directors may determine. One person may hold two or more Board offices, but no Board officer may act in more than one capacity where action of two or more officers is required.

6.02 Term of Office

Each officer shall serve a one-year term of office and may not serve more than three (3) consecutive terms of office. Unless unanimously elected by the Board at the end of his/her three (3) year terms or to fill a vacancy in an officer position, each Board officer's term of office shall begin upon the adjournment of the Board meeting at which elected and shall end upon the adjournment of the Board meeting during which a successor is elected.

6.03 Removal and Resignation

The Board of Directors may remove an officer at any time, with or without cause. Any officer may resign at any time by giving written notice to the corporation without prejudice to the rights, if any, of the corporation under any contract to which the officer is a party. Any resignation shall take effect at the date of the receipt of the notice or at any later time specified in the notice, unless otherwise specified in the notice. The acceptance of the resignation shall not be necessary to make it effective.

6.04 Board President

The Board President shall be the Chief Volunteer Officer of the corporation. The Board President shall lead the Board of Directors in performing its duties and responsibilities, including, if present, presiding at all meetings of the Board of Directors, and shall perform all other duties incident to the office or properly required by the Board of Directors.

6.05 Vice President

In the absence or disability of the Board President, the ranking Vice President or Vice President designated by the Board of Directors shall perform the duties of the Board President. When so acting, the Vice President shall have all the powers of and be subject to all the restrictions upon the Board President. The Vice President shall have such other powers and perform such other duties prescribed for them by the Board of Directors or the Board President. The Vice President shall normally accede to the office of Board President upon the completion of the Board President's term of office.

6.06 Secretary

The Secretary shall keep or cause to be kept a book of minutes of all meetings and actions of Directors and committees of Directors. The minutes of each meeting shall state the time and place that it was held and such other information as shall be necessary to determine the actions taken and whether the meeting was held in accordance with the law and these Bylaws. The Secretary shall cause notice to be given of all meetings of Directors and committees as required by the Bylaws. The Secretary shall have such other powers and perform such other duties as may be prescribed by the Board of Directors or the Board President. The Secretary may appoint, with approval of the Board, a Director to assist in performance of all or part of the duties of the Secretary.

6.07 Treasurer

The Treasurer shall be the lead Director for oversight of the financial condition and affairs of the corporation. The Treasurer shall oversee and keep the Board informed of the financial condition of the corporation and of audit or financial review results. In conjunction with other Directors or officers, the Treasurer shall oversee budget preparation and shall ensure that appropriate financial reports, including an account of major transactions and the financial condition of the corporation, are made available to the Board of Directors on a timely basis or as may be required by the Board of Directors. The Treasurer shall perform all duties properly required by the Board of Directors or the Board President. The Treasurer may appoint, with approval of the Board, a qualified fiscal agent or member of the staff to assist in performance of all or part of the duties of the Treasurer.

6.08 Non-Director Officers

The Board of Directors may designate additional officer positions of the corporation and may appoint and assign duties to other non-Director officers of the corporation.

ARTICLE VII

CONTRACTS, CHECKS, LOANS, INDEMNIFICATION AND RELATED MATTERS

7.01 Contracts and other Writings

Except as otherwise provided by resolution of the Board or Board policy, all contracts, deeds, leases, mortgages, grants, and other agreements of the corporation shall be executed on its behalf by the Treasurer or other persons to whom the corporation has delegated authority to execute such documents in accordance with policies approved by the Board.

7.02 Checks, Drafts

All checks, drafts, or other orders for payment of money, notes, or other evidence of indebtedness issued in the name of the corporation, shall be signed by such officer or officers, agent or agents, of the corporation and in such manner as shall from time to time be determined by resolution of the Board.

7.03 Deposits

All funds of the corporation not otherwise employed shall be deposited from time to time to the credit of the corporation in such banks, trust companies, or other depository as the Board or a designated committee of the Board may select.

7.04 Loans

No loans shall be contracted on behalf of the corporation and no evidence of indebtedness shall be issued in its name unless authorized by resolution of the Board. Such authority may be general or confined to specific instances.

7.05 Indemnification

a. Mandatory Indemnification. The corporation shall indemnify a Director or former Director, who was wholly successful, on the merits or otherwise, in the defense of any proceeding to which he or she was a party because he or she is or was a Director of the corporation against reasonable expenses incurred by him or her in connection with the proceedings.

b. Permissible Indemnification. The corporation shall indemnify a Director or former Director made a party to a proceeding because he or she is or was a Director of the corporation, against liability incurred in the proceeding, if the determination to indemnify him or her has been made in the manner prescribed by the law and payment has been authorized in the manner prescribed by law.

c. Advance for Expenses. Expenses incurred in defending a civil or criminal action, suit or proceeding may be paid by the corporation in advance of the final disposition of such action, suit or proceeding, as authorized by the Board of Directors in the specific case, upon receipt of (i) a written affirmation from the Director, officer, employee or agent of his or her good faith belief that he or she is entitled to indemnification as authorized in this Article, and (ii) an undertaking by or on behalf of the Director, officer, employee or agent to repay such amount, unless it shall ultimately be determined that he or she is entitled to be indemnified by the corporation in these Bylaws.

d. Indemnification of Officers, Agents and Employees. An officer of the corporation who is not a Director is entitled to mandatory indemnification under this Article to the same extent as a Director. The corporation may also indemnify and advance expenses to an employee or agent of the corporation who is not a Director, consistent with the law of the state in which the non-profit is incorporated and public policy, provided that such indemnification, and the scope of such indemnification, is set forth by the general or specific action of the Board or by contract.

ARTICLE VIII

MISCELLANEOUS

8.01 Books and Records

The corporation shall keep correct and complete books and records of account and shall keep minutes of the proceedings of all meetings of its Board of Directors, a record of all actions taken by Board of Directors without a meeting, and a record of all actions taken by committees of the Board. In addition, the corporation shall keep a copy of the corporation's Certificate of Formation and Bylaws as amended to date.

8.02 Fiscal Year

The fiscal year of the corporation shall be from January 1 to December 31 of each year.

8.03 Conflict of Interest

The Board shall adopt and periodically review a Conflict of Interest Policy to protect the corporation's interest when it is contemplating any transaction or arrangement which may benefit any Director, officer, employee, affiliate, or member of a committee with Board-delegated powers.

8.04 Nondiscrimination Policy

The officers, Directors, committee members, employees, and persons served by this corporation shall be selected entirely on a nondiscriminatory basis with respect to age, sex, race, religion, national origin, and sexual orientation. It is the policy of [insert the name of the non-profit] not to discriminate on the basis of race, creed, ancestry, marital status, gender, sexual orientation, age, physical disability, veteran's status, political service or affiliation, color, religion, or national origin.

8.05 Bylaw Amendment

These Bylaws may be amended, altered, repealed, or restated by a vote of the majority of the Board of Directors then in office at a meeting of the Board, provided, however,

a. that no amendment shall be made to these Bylaws which would cause the corporation to cease to qualify as an exempt corporation under Section 501 (c)(3) of the Internal Revenue Code of 1986, or the corresponding section of any future Federal tax code; and,

b. that an amendment does not affect the voting rights of Directors. An amendment that does affect the voting rights of Directors further requires ratification by [choose between "a majority" or "a two-thirds"] vote of a quorum of Directors at a Board meeting.

c. that all amendments be consistent with the Certificate of Formation.

ARTICLE IX

COUNTERTERRORISM AND DUE DILIGENCE POLICY

In furtherance of its exemption by contributions to other organizations, domestic or foreign, [insert the name of the non-profit] shall stipulate how the funds will be used and shall require the recipient to provide the corporation with detailed records and financial proof of how the funds were utilized.

Although adherence and compliance with the U.S. Department of the Treasury's publication entitled the "Voluntary Best Practice for U.S.-Based Charities," is not mandatory, [insert the name of the non-profit] willfully and voluntarily recognizes and puts to practice these guidelines and suggestions to reduce, develop, re-evaluate and strengthen a risk-based approach to guard against the threat of diversion of charitable funds or exploitation of charitable activity by terrorist organizations and their support networks.

[Insert the name of the non-profit] shall also comply and put into practice the federal guidelines, suggestion, laws and limitation set forth by pre-existing U.S. legal requirements related to combating terrorist financing, which include, but are not limited to, various sanctions programs administered by the Office of Foreign Assets Control (OFAC) in regard to its foreign activities.

ARTICLE X

DOCUMENT RETENTION POLICY

10.01 Purpose

The purpose of this Document Retention Policy is to establish standards for document integrity, retention, and destruction, and to promote the proper treatment of [insert the name of the non-profit]'s records.

10.02 Policy

Section 1. General Guidelines. Records should not be kept if they are no longer needed for the operation of the business or required by law. Unnecessary records should be eliminated from the files. The cost of maintaining records is an expense which can grow unreasonably if good housekeeping is not performed. A mass of records also makes it more difficult to find pertinent records. [Optional: Where possible, the non-profit shall adopt a digital, non-paper filing and retention system.]

From time to time, [insert the name of the non-profit] may establish retention or destruction policies or schedules for specific categories of records in order to ensure legal compliance, and also to accomplish other objectives, such as preserving intellectual property and cost management. Several categories of documents that warrant special consideration are identified below. While minimum retention periods are established, the retention of the documents identified below and of documents not included in the identified categories should be determined primarily by the application of the general guidelines affecting document retention, as well as the exception for litigation relevant documents and any other pertinent factors.

Section 2. Exception for Litigation Relevant Documents. [insert the name of the non-profit] expects all officers, Directors, and employees to comply fully with any published records retention or destruction policies and schedules, provided that all officers, Directors, and employees should note the following general exception to any stated destruction schedule: If you believe, or the [insert the name of the non-profit] informs you, that corporate records are relevant to litigation, or potential litigation (i.e. a dispute that could result in litigation), then you must preserve those records until it is determined that the records are no longer needed. That exception supersedes any previously or subsequently established destruction schedule for those records.

Section 3. Minimum Retention Periods for Specific Categories

a. Corporate Documents. Corporate records include the corporation's Certificate of Formation, Bylaws and IRS Form 1023 and Application for Exemption. Corporate records should be retained permanently. IRS regulations require that the Form 1023 be available for public inspection upon request.

b. Tax Records. Tax records include, but may not be limited to, documents concerning payroll, expenses, proof of contributions made by donors, accounting procedures, and other documents concerning the corporation's revenues. Tax records should be retained for at least seven (7) years from the date of filing the applicable return.

c. Employment Records/Personnel Records. State and federal statutes require the corporation to keep certain recruitment, employment and personnel information. The corporation should also keep personnel files that reflect performance reviews and any complaints brought against the corporation or individual employees under applicable state and federal statutes. The corporation should also keep in the employee's personnel file all final memoranda and correspondence reflecting performance reviews and actions taken by or against personnel. Employment applications should be retained for three (3) years. Retirement and pension records should be kept permanently. Other employment and personnel records should be retained for seven years.

d. Board and Board Committee Materials. Meeting minutes should be retained in perpetuity in the corporation's minute book. A clean copy of all other Board and Board Committee materials should be kept for no less than three (3) years by the corporation.

e. Press Releases/Public Filings. The corporation should retain permanent copies of all press releases and publicly filed documents under the theory that the corporation should have its own copy to test the accuracy of any document a member of the public can theoretically produce against the corporation.

f. Legal Files. Legal counsel should be consulted to determine the retention period of particular documents, but legal documents should generally be maintained for a period of ten (10) years.

g. Marketing and Sales Documents. The corporation should keep final copies of marketing and sales documents for the same period of time it keeps other corporate files, generally three (3) years. An exception to the three-year policy may be sales invoices, contracts, leases, licenses, and other legal documentation. These documents should be kept for at least three (3) years beyond the life of the agreement.

h. Development/Intellectual Property and Trade Secrets. Development documents are often subject to intellectual property protection in their final form (e.g., patents, trademarks, service marks, and copyrights). The documents detailing the development process are often also of value to the corporation and are protected as a trade secret where the corporation:

    i. derives independent economic value from the secrecy of the information; and

    ii. has taken affirmative steps to keep the information confidential.

The corporation should keep all documents designated as containing trade secret information for at least the life of the trade secret.

i. Contracts. Final, execution copies of all contracts entered into by the corporation should be retained. The corporation should retain copies of the final contracts for at least three (3) years beyond the life of the agreement, and longer in the case of publicly filed contracts.

j. Correspondence. Unless correspondence falls under another category listed elsewhere in this policy, correspondence should generally be saved for two (2) years.

k. Banking and Accounting. Accounts payable ledgers and schedules should be kept for seven (7) years. Bank reconciliations, bank statements, deposit slips and checks (unless for important payments and purchases) should be kept for three (3) years. Any inventories of products, materials, and supplies and any invoices should be kept for seven (7) years.

l. Insurance. Expired insurance policies, insurance records, accident reports, claims, etc. should be kept permanently.

m. Audit Records. External audit reports should be kept permanently. Internal audit reports should be kept for three (3) years.

Section 4. Electronic Mail. E-mail that needs to be saved should be either:

i. printed in hard copy and kept in the appropriate file; or

ii. downloaded to a computer file and kept electronically or on disk as a separate file. The retention period depends upon the subject matter of the e-mail, as covered elsewhere in this policy.

ARTICLE XI

Transparency and Accountability

Disclosure of Financial Information With The General Public

11.01 Purpose

By making full and accurate information about its mission, activities, finances, and governance publicly available, [insert the name of the non-profit] practices and encourages transparency and accountability to the general public. This Policy will:

a. indicate which documents and materials produced by the corporation are presumptively open to staff and/or the public,

b. indicate which documents and materials produced by the corporation are presumptively closed to staff and/or the public, and

c.   specify the procedures whereby the open/closed status of documents and materials can be altered.

The details of this Policy are as follow:

11.02 Financial and IRS documents (form 1023 and the form 990). [insert the name of the non-profit] shall provide its Internal Revenue forms 990, 990-T, 1023 and 5227, Bylaws, Conflict of Interest Policy, and financial statements to the general public for inspection free of charge.

11.03 Means and Conditions of Disclosure

[Insert the name of the non-profit] shall make "Widely Available" the aforementioned documents on its internet website [insert url for non-profit website] to be viewed and inspected by the general public.

a.   The documents shall be posted in a format that allows an individual using the Internet to access, download, view and print them in a manner that exactly reproduces the image of the original document filed with the IRS (except information exempt from public disclosure requirements, such as contributor lists).

b.   The website shall clearly inform readers that the document is available and provide instructions for downloading it.

c.   [Insert the name of the non-profit] shall not charge a fee for downloading the information. Documents shall not be posted in a format that would require special computer hardware or software (other than software readily available to the public free of charge).

d.   [Insert the name of the non-profit] shall inform anyone requesting the information where this information can be found, including the web address. This information must be provided immediately for in-person requests and within 7 (7) days for mailed requests.

11.04 IRS Annual Information Returns (Form 990)

[Insert the name of the non-profit] shall submit the Form 990 to its Board of Directors prior to the filing of the Form 990. While neither the approval of the Form 990 or a review of the 990 is required under federal law, the corporation's Form 990 shall be submitted to each member of the Board of Director's via hard copy or email at least ten (10) days before the Form 990 is filed with the IRS.

11.05 Board

a. All Board deliberations shall be open to the public except where the Board passes a motion to make any specific portion confidential.
b. All Board minutes shall be open to the public once accepted by the Board, except where the Board passes a motion to make any specific portion confidential.
c. All papers and materials considered by the Board shall be open to the public following the meeting at which they are considered, except where the Board passes a motion to make any specific paper or material confidential.

11.06 Staff Records

a. All staff records shall be available for consultation by the staff member concerned or by their legal representatives.
b. No staff records shall be made available to any person outside the corporation except the authorized governmental agencies.
c. Within the corporation, staff records shall be made available only to those persons with managerial or personnel responsibilities for that staff member, except that
d. Staff records shall be made available to the Board when requested.

11.07 Donor Records

a. All donor records shall be available for consultation by the members and donors concerned or by their legal representatives.
b. No donor records shall be made available to any other person outside the corporation except the authorized governmental agencies.
c. Within the corporation, donor records shall be made available only to those persons with managerial or personnel responsibilities for dealing with those donors, except that donor records shall be made available to the Board when requested.

ARTICLE XII

CODES OF ETHICS AND WHISTLEBLOWER POLICY

12.01 Purpose

[Insert the name of the non-profit] requires and encourages Directors, officers and employees to observe and practice high standards of business and personal ethics in the conduct of their duties and responsibilities. The employees and representatives of the corporation must practice honesty and integrity in fulfilling their responsibilities and comply with all applicable laws and regulations. It is the intent of [insert the name of the non-profit] to adhere to all laws and regulations that apply to the corporation and the underlying purpose of this policy is to support the corporation's goal of legal compliance. The support of all corporate staff is necessary to achieving compliance with various laws and regulations.

12.02 Reporting Violations

If any Director, officer, staff or employee reasonably believes that some policy, practice, or activity of [insert the name of the non-profit] is in violation of law, a written complaint must be filed by that person with the Vice President or the Board President.

12.03 Acting in Good Faith

Anyone filing a complaint concerning a violation or suspected violation of a law or regulation must be acting in good faith and have reasonable grounds for believing the information disclosed indicates a violation. Any allegations that prove not to be substantiated and which prove to have been made maliciously or knowingly to be false shall be viewed as a serious disciplinary offense.

12.04 Retaliation

A person filing the aforesaid complaint is protected from retaliation only if she/he brings the alleged unlawful activity, policy, or practice to the attention of [insert the name of the non-profit] and provides the [insert the name of the non-profit] with a reasonable opportunity to investigate and correct the alleged unlawful activity. The protection described below is only available to individuals that comply with this requirement.

[Insert the name of the non-profit] shall not retaliate against any Director, officer, staff or employee who in good faith, has made a protest or raised a complaint against some practice of [insert the name of the non-profit] or of another individual or entity with whom [insert the name of the non-profit] has a business relationship, on the basis of a reasonable belief that the practice is in violation of law, or a clear mandate of public policy.

[Insert the name of the non-profit] shall not retaliate against any Director, officer, staff or employee who discloses or threatens to disclose to a supervisor or a public body, any activity, policy, or practice of [insert the name of the non-profit] that the individual reasonably believes is in violation of a law, or a rule, or regulation mandated pursuant to law or is in violation of a clear mandate of public policy concerning the health, safety, welfare, or protection of the environment.

12.05 Confidentiality

Violations or suspected violations may be submitted on a confidential basis by the complainant or may be submitted anonymously. Reports of violations or suspected violations shall be kept confidential to the extent possible, consistent with the need to conduct an adequate investigation.

12.06 Handling of Reported Violations

The Board President or Vice President shall notify the sender and acknowledge receipt of the reported violation or suspected violation within five business days. All reports shall be promptly investigated by the Board and its appointed committee and appropriate corrective action shall be taken if warranted by the investigation.

This policy shall be made available to all Directors, officers, staffs or employees and they shall have the opportunity to ask questions about the policy.

ARTICLE XIII

AMENDMENT OF Certificate of Formation

13.01 Amendment

Any amendment to the Certificate of Formation may be adopted by approval of two-thirds (2/3) of the Board of Directors.

CERTIFICATE OF ADOPTION OF BYLAWS

I do hereby certify that the above stated Bylaws of [insert the name of the non-profit] were approved by the [insert name of non-profit]'s Board of Directors on [insert date] and constitute a complete copy of the Bylaws of the corporation.

Secretary _____

Date: _____

CHAPTER 11

DEVELOP A CONFLICT OF INTEREST POLICY

"Opportunities don't happen, you create them."

—Chris Grosser

SET PERSONAL INTERESTS ASIDE

IRS is concerned about conflicts of interest within 501(c) (3) corporations. A conflict of interest occurs when someone in a responsible position within a nonprofit has competing interests and is faced with making choices that could benefit themselves (or friends and family members) to the detriment of the organization. Board members and directors of a nonprofit have a first duty to promote the best interest of the organization. They must lay their personal interests aside when conducting the business of the nonprofit. Should a conflict of interest arise, it should be disclosed immediately.

Below is a sample conflict of interest policy from IRS containing the minimum requirements. It is for a health care organization. You can change to it to meet your organizational needs. In addition, IRS wants board members and directors to fill out an annual Conflict of Interest Disclosure statement which should be kept on file with the corporation's other important documents. If you do not want to modify and type out the sample Conflict of Interest Policy, or develop a Conflict of Interest Annual Statement, free templates come with the Certificate of Formation and Bylaws package on my website at www.doyourownnonprofit.com

IRS SAMPLE CONFLICT OF INTEREST POLICY

ARTICLE I

Purpose

The purpose of the conflict of interest policy is to protect this tax-exempt organization's (Organization) interest when it is contemplating entering into a transaction or arrangement that might benefit the private interest of an officer or director of the Organization or might result in a possible excess benefit transaction. This policy is intended to supplement but not replace any applicable state and federal laws governing conflict of interest applicable to nonprofit and charitable organizations.

ARTICLE II

Definitions

1. Interested Person

Any director, principal officer, or member of a committee with governing board delegated powers, who has a direct or indirect financial interest, as defined below, is an interested person.

If a person is an interested person with respect to any entity in the health care system of which the organization is a part, he or she is an interested person with respect to all entities in the health care system.

2. Financial Interest

A person has a financial interest if the person has, directly or indirectly, through business, investment, or family:

a. An ownership or investment interest in any entity with which the Organization has a transaction or arrangement,

b. A compensation arrangement with the Organization or with any entity or individual with which the Organization has a transaction or arrangement, or

c. A potential ownership or investment interest in, or compensation arrangement with, any entity or individual with which the Organization is negotiating a transaction or arrangement.

Compensation includes direct and indirect remuneration as well as gifts or favors that are not insubstantial. A financial interest is not necessarily a conflict of interest. Under Article III, Section 2, a person who has a financial interest may have a conflict of interest only if the appropriate governing board or committee decides that a conflict of interest exists.

ARTICLE III

Procedures

1. *Duty to Disclose*

In connection with any actual or possible conflict of interest, an interested person must disclose the existence of the financial interest and be given the opportunity to disclose all material facts to the directors and members of committees with governing board delegated powers considering the proposed transaction or arrangement.

2. *Determining Whether a Conflict of Interest Exists*

After disclosure of the financial interest and all material facts, and after any discussion with the interested person, he/she shall leave the governing board or committee meeting while the determination of a conflict of interest is discussed and voted upon. The remaining board or committee members shall decide if a conflict of interest exists.

3. *Procedures for Addressing the Conflict of Interest*

a. An interested person may make a presentation at the governing board or committee meeting, but after the presentation, he/she shall leave the meeting during the discussion of, and the vote on, the transaction or arrangement involving the possible conflict of interest.

b. The chairperson of the governing board or committee shall, if appropriate, appoint a disinterested person or committee to investigate alternatives to the proposed transaction or arrangement.

c. After exercising due diligence, the governing board or committee shall determine whether the Organization can obtain with reasonable efforts a more advantageous transaction or arrangement from a person or entity that would not give rise to a conflict of interest.

d. If a more advantageous transaction or arrangement is not reasonably possible under circumstances not producing a conflict of interest, the governing board or committee shall determine by a majority vote of the disinterested directors whether the transaction or arrangement is in the Organization's best interest, for its own benefit, and whether it is fair and reasonable. In conformity with the above determination it shall make its decision as to whether to enter into the transaction or arrangement.

4. *Violations of the Conflicts of Interest Policy*

a. If the governing board or committee has reasonable cause to believe a member has failed to disclose actual or possible conflicts of interest, it shall inform the member of the basis for such belief and afford the member an opportunity to explain the alleged failure to disclose.

b. If, after hearing the member's response and after making further investigation as warranted by the circumstances, the governing board or committee determines the member has failed to disclose an actual or possible conflict of interest, it shall take appropriate disciplinary and corrective action.

ARTICLE IV

Records of Proceedings

The minutes of the governing board and all committees with board delegated powers shall contain:

a. The names of the persons who disclosed or otherwise were found to have a financial interest in connection with an actual or possible conflict of interest, the nature of the financial interest, any action taken to determine whether a conflict of interest was present, and the governing board or committee's decision as to whether a conflict of interest in fact existed.

b. The names of the persons who were present for discussions and votes relating to the transaction or arrangement, the content of the discussion, including any alternatives to the proposed transaction or arrangement, and a record of any votes taken in connection with the proceedings.

ARTICLE V

Compensation

a. A voting member of the governing board who receives compensation, directly or indirectly, from the Organization for services is precluded from voting on matters pertaining to that member's compensation.

b. A voting member of any committee whose jurisdiction includes compensation matters and who receives compensation, directly or indirectly, from the Organization for services is precluded from voting on matters pertaining to that member's compensation.

c. No voting member of the governing board or any committee whose jurisdiction includes compensation matters and who receives compensation, directly or indirectly, from the Organization, either individually or collectively, is prohibited from providing information to any committee regarding compensation.

ARTICLE VI

Annual Statements

Each director, principal officer and member of a committee with governing board delegated powers shall annually sign a statement which affirms such person:

a. Has received a copy of the conflicts of interest policy,
b. Has read and understands the policy,
c. Has agreed to comply with the policy, and
d. Understands the Organization is charitable and in order to maintain its federal tax exemption it must engage primarily in activities which accomplish one or more of its tax-exempt purposes.

ARTICLE VII

Periodic Reviews

To ensure the Organization operates in a manner consistent with charitable purposes and does not engage in activities that could jeopardize its tax-exempt status, periodic reviews shall be conducted. The periodic reviews shall, at a minimum, include the following subjects:

a. Whether compensation arrangements and benefits are reasonable, based on competent survey information and the result of arm's length bargaining.

b. Whether partnerships, joint ventures, and arrangements with management organizations conform to the Organization's written policies, are properly recorded, reflect reasonable investment or payments for goods and services, further charitable purposes and do not result in inurnment, impermissible private benefit or in an excess benefit transaction.

ARTICLE VIII

Use of Outside Experts

When conducting the periodic reviews as provided for in Article VII, the Organization may, but need not, use outside advisors. If outside experts are used, their use shall not relieve the governing board of its responsibility for ensuring periodic reviews are conducted.

Now that the conflict of interest matters are take care of, it's time to lay out plans for the first board of directors meeting.

.

CHAPTER 12

HOLD AND DOCUMENT THE FIRST BOARD MEETING

"You miss 100% of the shots you don't take."

—Wayne Gretzky

MINUTES ARE LEGAL DOCUMENTS

Did you know that IRS and auditors consider board meeting minutes as legal documents that will hold up in court? Many people believe that if it's not in the meeting minutes, it didn't occur, because the meeting minutes are the formal record of the business conducted and the decisions made by an organization.

There is no set format for meeting minutes and each organization should decide how the meeting minutes should look. When secretaries of the board change, the format often changes as well to suit the new secretary. As long as the required information is recorded, the format is not critical. Copies of meeting minutes from previous meetings should be given to board members for review and approval. All meeting minutes should be filed in a safe accessible place.

WHAT SHOULD BE INCLUDED

There are some things that should be included in every set of meeting minutes:

1. Name of the organization
2. Date and time of the meeting
3. Who ran the meeting?
4. Who was there and who was absent
5. What was voted on and whether anyone abstained from voting
6. All motions made
7. When the meeting ended
8. Who prepared the meeting minutes.

Personal opinions and heated arguments or discussions should not be included. Minutes should cover the business of the organization, not document disagreements among members. Also do not include in-depth details of reports. It's better to simply attach the reports to the minutes.

FIRST BOARD MEETING

If you are about to conduct your first board meeting, you want to include the business of setting up the organization and getting it running. Your meeting minutes should include the following:

1. Who is on the initial board of directors?
2. How you will elect or appoint board members in the future
3. Approve application for an FEIN number (if not already done)
4. Approve development of Certificate of Formation (if not already done)
5. Adopt the organization's bylaws
6. Approve applying for 501(c) (3) status with IRS
7. Approve setting up banking accounts and decide how funds will be handled

8. Approve the Conflict of Interest policy
9. Determine fiscal accounting year

A free template of first board meeting minutes is included in the Certificate of Formation and Bylaws package at www.doyourownnonprofit.com

At this meeting, most of the preliminary matters have been taken care of. It's now time to learn about the forms needed to attain your 501 (c) (3) status.

PART II

IRS FORM 1023
APPLICATION FOR
TAX EXEMPT STATUS

CHAPTER 13

REQUEST FOR RECOGNITION OF EXEMPTION

"Whether you think you can or you think you can't, you're right."

—Henry Ford

WHERE TO BEGIN

If you have completed all the requirements in the previous chapters, you're ready to complete the IRS Form 1023, *Request for Recognition of Exemption under Section 501(c) (3) of the Internal Revenue Code.* You can get a copy of the form to fill out online and print at www.irs.gov and search for Form 1023.

WHAT TO EXPECT

It takes several months to hear back from IRS after filing. If you provide complete information on your application, and any required accompanying schedules, you'll probably hear back from them within 3 months.

If your application contains everything IRS needs to know, a determination letter will be issued. If not, you will receive requests for additional clarification or information. Needing more information can significantly delay approval. Once the application is approved, it will be effective as of the original date of the application you sent in, or the date the state approved your articles of organization if you desire.

You can get expedited handling if you request it for a compelling reason. Good compelling reasons might include:

- Pending grants that will not be made without 501(c) (3) status;
- Your organization is created to provide relief to victims of disasters such as recent floods, hurricanes, tsunamis, or tornadoes
- Your application has been delayed because of problems at IRS due to no fault of your organization

IRS estimates that it takes over 100 hours to complete the 501(c) (3) process. Hopefully this book will cut down those hours by half or more. But get ready to dig in, and describe your organization completely to IRS so that a quick determination can be made without required follow up from IRS. If you put in the work up front to do it right the first time, you'll not have to deal with ongoing correspondence and paperwork from IRS. Also if you use examples from the narratives in Appendix A, you can cut that time down to one or two day's effort.

DISCLOSURE

Here's an interesting tip that most people do not know. You are allowed to see a copy of the Form 1023 for most nonprofit organizations that have been approved after July 15, 1987. You can be charged a fair price for making copies. Not all organizations know they are required to disclose their applications. You can ask for a copy of the paperwork and quote the IRS guidance (do an internet search for Public Disclosure and Availability of Exempt Organizations Returns and Applications: Documents Subject to Public Disclosure) which states as of April 28, 2013:

An exempt organization must make available for public inspection its exemption application. An exemption application includes the Form 1023 (for organizations recognized as exempt under Internal Revenue Code Section 501(c) (3)), Form 1024 (for organizations recognized as exempt under most other paragraphs of Section 501(c)), or the letter submitted under the paragraphs for which no form is prescribed, together with supporting documents and any letter or document issued by the IRS concerning the application. A political organization exempt from taxation under Section 527(a) must make available for public inspection and copying its notice of status, Form 8871.

In addition, an exempt organization must make available for public inspection and copying its annual return. Such returns include Form 990, *Return of Organization Exempt from Income Tax*; Form 990-EZ, *Short Form Return of Organization Exempt from Income Tax*; Form 990-PF, *Return of Private Foundation*; Form 990-BL, *Information and Initial Excise Tax Return for Black Lung Benefit Trusts and Certain Related Persons*; and the Form 1065, *U.S. Partnership Return of Income.*

A Section 501(c) (3) organization must make available for public inspection and copying any Form 990-T *Exempt Organization Business Income Tax Return*, filed after August 17, 2006. Returns must be available for a three-year period beginning with the due date of the return (including any extension of time for filing). For this purpose, the *return* includes any schedules, attachments, or supporting documents that relate to the imposition of tax on the unrelated business income of the charitable organization.

An exempt organization is not required to disclose Schedule K-1 of Form 1065 or Schedule A of Form 990-BL. With the exception of private foundations, an exempt organization is not required to disclose the name and address of any contributor to the organization.

Many organizations meet the disclosure requirements by putting their public documents online. Some of those websites for approved nonprofits are contained in Appendix A to this book so you can look at actual paperwork and get a feel for what goes in each section and in the narrative of Form 1023. Seeing how others have handled the paperwork should remove some of the anxious feelings you might have about this part of the process.

If you have made it this far, you have all the preliminary requirements out of the way and you are ready to dig into the IRS application. Let's get started.

> **NOTE:** On July 1, 2014, IRS added Form 1023-EZ, *Streamlined Application for Recognition of Exemption under Section 501(c)(3) of the Internal Revenue Code,* for smaller organizations to simplify filing. It must be filed online, the cost is $400, and you must complete the Eligibility Checklist (which is 5 pages but not difficult). This is great news for small nonprofits because the Form 1023-EZ is only 3 pages compared to the Form 1023, which is 26 pages. Eligibility worksheet is located at http://www.irs.gov/pub/irs-pdf/i1023ez.pdf after the instructions. There are many restrictions on use of this new form and many types of nonprofits are not eligible.

To be eligible to use the Form 1023-EZ, you must meet ALL these requirements:

1. Less than $50,000 gross receipts for the past three years and projected for the next three years
2. Less than $250,000 in assets
3. Formed in the U. S. and have a U. S. mailing address (or U. S. territory)
4. Must not be a successor to, or controlled by, an entity suspended under section 501(p) terrorist organization
5. Cannot be a limited liability corporation (LLC)
6. Cannot be successor to a for-profit entity

7. Must not have been previously revoked for failing to file Form 990-series for 3 years and applying for retroactive reinstatement

8. Must not be a church, convention, or association of churches

9. Must not be a school, college, university, or cooperative service organization for an educational institution

10. Must not be a hospital, medical research organization, or cooperative hospital service organization

11. Must not be a qualified charitable risk pool

12. Must not be a supporting organization to other nonprofits

13. Must not be credit counseling or consumer credit services

14. Cannot invest 5% or more of your total assets in securities or funds that are not publicly traded

15. Not participate, or intend to participate, in partnerships (including entities treated as partnerships for federal tax purposes) in which you share profits and losses with partners other than section 501(c)(3) organizations

16. Cannot sell carbon credits or carbon offsets

17. Must not be an HMO

18. Cannot engage in Accountable Care Organization (ACO) activities

19. Cannot maintain donor advised funds

20. Cannot be testing for public safety

21. Must not be a private operating foundation

The remaining chapters of the book contain instructions for filling out Form 1023. If you are eligible to use the streamlined Form 1023-EZ, those instructions can help you fill out the streamlined form.

Here is a rundown of the sections of Form 1023-EZ with comments to help you answer the questions:

Part 1: Identification of Applicant. The new form combines Part I and Part V of Form 1023, but eliminates many questions. It is much faster to fill out than the long form.

Part II: Organizational Structure. Most organizations will be corporations and the organizing document is the Articles of Incorporation, but in Texas it is called Certificate of Formation. You must be able to check the boxes in questions 5, 6, and 7 for approval. If you used the document templates in earlier chapters, you have no problem checking these boxes.

Part III:

Question 1: NTEE Code is a 3 character code that describes your activities. A list of NTEE codes can be found on pages 18 – 20 of the Form 1023-EZ instructions, which are located online at http://www.irs.gov/pub/irs-pdf/i1023ez.pdf

Question 2: Most organizations are charitable. Remember that you are not eligible to use Form 1023-EZ if you are a school or church organization, or test for public safety.

Question 3: You must be able to check the box attesting that you will not violate the rules.

Question 4: Best if you can answer "no." Stops questions, delays, and filing Form 5768.

Question 5: Remember your organization's gross receipts are less than $50,000 to qualify to use this form, so compensation paid, if any, should be proportionate.

Question 6: Reimbursing employee business expenses does not count when considering this question.

Question 7: It is perfectly fine to conduct activities and provide grants and assistance to individuals and organizations outside the United States, as long as it is for tax exempt purposes.

Question 8: Tricky question. If you answer "yes," your application may be delayed pending further inquiry from IRS.

Question 9: If you answer "yes," you must fill out an additional tax return at the end of the year, Form 990-T for the unrelated business income.

Question 10: Bingo and other gaming activities have many restrictions and safeguards from the state and federal government. Could delay your application if IRS needs more information. For more information, see Publication 3079, Tax-Exempt Organizations and Gaming.

Question 11: If you provide disaster relief, mark "yes," and see Publication 3833, Disaster Relief: Providing Assistance through Charitable Organizations.

Part IV: Foundation Classification. Most organizations will check 1a.

Part V: If you use this application, your effective date will not be retroactive to the day you were revoked. When you check the box, you are saying you did not fail to file intentionally, and that you have made changes to keep it from happening again. There are 3 conditions you must meet to use this form for reinstatement: It must be the first time you were revoked, you must have been eligible to file Form 990-N (electronic postcard return) or Form 990-EZ (short form return), and you must file within 15 months of being revoked.

Go to www.pay.gov and register. Enter 1023-EZ in the search box, and complete the form. You can set up a deduction from your bank account or use a credit card to pay the application fee.

If you cannot use the Form 1023-EZ, you will need to use the long form, Form 1023. Instructions for completing that form start in the next chapter.

CHAPTER 14:
PART I

IDENTIFICATION OF APPLICANT

"Ask and it will be given to you; search, and you will find; knock and the door will be opened for you."

—Jesus

TAKE IT ONE STEP AT A TIME

You are now at the point where you will begin filling out the actual application. No need to be overwhelmed – simply take it one step at a time and you will get through this.

NOTE: If you are unsure of what to put in any section of the Form 1023, call IRS Tax Exempt and Government Entities Customer Account Services at (877) 829-5500. Better to ask now than to delay the approval of your application for months.

Start by pulling up the online application at http://www.irs.gov/pub/irs-pdf/f1023.pdf

A good rule of thumb is to work on the application in sections, save it to your computer, and then come back and add to it later. I strongly suggest that you print a copy of all completed sections as you finish them. This is just in case your computer malfunctions, or for some reason the online document does not save your answers the way it should. That way you will not have come up with the answers again. (Work smart – take all necessary precautions.)

Below I have listed exactly what is needed for each specific line in the application:

Line 1: Full name of organization (exactly as it appears in your organizing document)

Enter your organization's name from Articles of Incorporation or similar document, including amendments. The name on your FEIN confirmation should match as well.

Line 2: c/o Name

If you want a specific person to be the go-to person for correspondence, put in an *in-care-of* name here. If you are the founder and are using your personal address, you can use your name. You can also leave it blank.

Line 3: Mailing address

This will be the address you want correspondence sent to. A post office box is fine if that is where you get your mail. (For overseas addresses, list information in this order: city, province or state, and fully-spelled-out country, followed by the customary postal code for the country.)

Line 4: Employer Identification Number (EIN)

Enter the FEIN given to you by IRS. It is 9-digits long. The first 2 digits, a dash, and the last 7 digits. For example, the EIN for Pasture

Valley Children Missions (a nonprofit I founded) is 35-2468924. If you do not have an FEIN number, go back to Chapter 4 and follow the directions. You can get a number over the phone from IRS. IRS no longer accepts applications for organizations without FEIN numbers.

Line 5: Month the annual accounting period ends (01-12)

Your accounting year should end at a logical point. For example, a school organization may end June 30 or July 31. Most other organizations will have a December 31 accounting period end. Put the month in which you plan to end your annual accounting period. The last day of the accounting period will be the last day of the month you select. Also check your bylaws to verify the accounting period. Depending on the month you select, your first accounting period may be less than one calendar year. For example, if you start your nonprofit in May and your accounting year ends in December, you will only have a seven month accounting period the first year. This is not a problem.

Line 6a: Primary contact

Who do you want IRS to talk with if they need to discuss your application, organizational documents, bylaws, or other such matters? This person can be an officer, director, or any other person you designate to discuss your organization's rules and procedures. It can also be you. Another option is to designate an authorized representative, attorney, or accountant to represent you by filing an IRS Form 2848 with your application.

Line 6b: Phone

What is the contact person's phone number? Include the area code.

Line 6c: Fax (optional)

Enter fax number if you have one.

Line 7

If you have authorized an attorney or accountant to talk with IRS on your behalf, check "Yes" and attach IRS Form 2848. If your contact is you or a member of your organization in some facet, check "No."

Line 8

Is there anyone outside your organization that you have paid or promised to pay to:

- Help you fill out your Form 1023?
- Help you establish your organization?
- Set up fundraising programs?
- Handle tax matters?
- Prepare financials?
- Handle other organizational matters?

If you mark "Yes," you must provide the person's name, the name and address of the firm they represent, how much you paid or are going to pay, and exactly what the person has done or is doing. If not, then mark "No."

Line 9a: Organization's Website

If you have a website, list it here. The information you have on your actual website must match the information you include in this application. If you do not have a website, put in N/A. Also, if any other websites have your information on them or are maintained on your behalf, list them.

Line 9b: Email (optional)

If you want educational materials sent to you by IRS, give an email address if you have one. They will not contact you with confidential information by email, but will use U.S. Postal Service or fax. You do not have to include an email address.

Line 10

This item has to do with whether you will be required to file an annual information return using some version of Form 990. If you are a church, certain church affiliated organizations, or certain affiliates of government units, you are not required to file a Form 990. Include an explanation in the narrative section of why you do not think you need to file one of the versions of Form 990.

Private foundations must file a Form 990-PF regardless of gross receipts. For small budget organizations, you can do your information return online quickly. As long as you keep good records, it is not difficult to comply with the Form 990 requirement, especially if you set up your books using the same categories as are contained on the Form 990. Many grant-making organizations check to see that you are filing a Form 990 before they will accept or approve your application for a grant.

Failure to file a required Form 990 return for three years (in whatever version you must use) results in automatic revocation of 501(c) (3) status. When this occurs, you have 15 months to file your application all over again (and pay the fees again) to get your status back retroactive to the date of revocation.

If you file after 15 months from being revoked, you lose tax exempt status for the time you were revoked and the donations made to your organization during the time of revocation are not tax deductible to your donors.

Line 11

What date is on Articles of Incorporation? That is the date you use. If you choose to use an earlier date because you have been conducting business, you can request an earlier date. Just be aware that you must file for 501(c) (3) status within 27 months of beginning operations.

Line 12

Was your organization formed in another country outside the U.S.? Organizations formed in United States territories or possessions, Indian tribal or Alaska Native governments, or Washington, D.C. are considered domestic, not foreign. If you check "Yes," you must list the foreign country your organization was formed in. Otherwise, check "No."

Now that wasn't too painful, was it? In the next chapter you'll fill out all the information needed regarding your organizational structure.

CHAPTER 15: PART II

ORGANIZATIONAL STRUCTURE

"Everything you've ever wanted is on the other side of fear."
—George Addair

This section of the application has to do with your organizational structure. Your organization must be a corporation (including a limited liability corporation), or a trust in order to be eligible for 501(c) (3) status. In this section, you must select your form of organization and attach your organizing documents to the application.

Line 1: Corporation

IRS defines a corporation as:

> *"An entity organized under a Federal or state statute, or a statute of a federally recognized Indian tribal or Alaskan native government."*

This is the most popular and frequent organizational structure for 501(c) (3) status. You document your corporate status by filing your Articles of Incorporation. The state gives you back a certification of filing that includes the date you became a corporate entity. You must include an exact copy of your filed document with the Form 1023, as well as any amendments to the original document.

If you do not have an exact copy, you can contact your Secretary of State for another copy (recommended), or you can include a substitute copy either handwritten, typed, or printed, or otherwise reproduced. If you substitute, you must include a statement signed by a corporate officer that it is a complete and correct copy of the actual organizing document. You could use this declaration:

"I, _____ (name), _____ (office you hold), declare under penalty of law that this is a complete and correct copy of the articles of incorporation and that it contains all the powers, principles, purposes, functions, and other provisions by which we currently govern ourselves."

Line 2: Limited Liability Corporation

Not all Limited Liability Corporations or Companies are eligible for 501(c) (3) status. To qualify, all the membership of an LLC must be other 501(c) (3) agencies. LLC companies made up of individuals are not eligible for tax exempt status. LLCs are owned by members; nonprofit organizations are not owned, they are separate entities. This structure of organization is confusing, contradictory, and brings problems you may not want to try to solve. If you are contemplating LLC structure, contact an attorney for further guidance to avoid laborious paperwork with IRS and extended timeframes for approval, or rejection of your application.

Line 3: Unincorporated Association

An unincorporated association must have a written agreement laying out the purpose of the association. There must be at least two members. According to IRS instructions, "the articles of organization of an unincorporated association must include the name of your organization, your purpose, the date the document was adopted, and the signatures of at least two individuals." Date of adoption is important to IRS.

Line 4a: Trust

A trust can be established by a will or by a trust agreement or declaration of trust. If created by a will, a copy of the death certificate and a copy of pertinent parts of the will must be attached to the application. A trust involves three groups of people:

- The donor(s)
- The trustee(s)
- The beneficiaries

Trustees can be sued on behalf of the trust. Not all trust instruments and structures are eligible for 501(c) (3) status.

Line 4b: Have You Been Funded?

For a trust to exist, it must be funded with money or real or personal property to be legal.

Line 5: Bylaws

If you have bylaws, attach them. IRS does not require them, but if you do not have them, some of their questions about how you function as an organization will not be answered. In that case, they may not approve your application without further information. This could delay your application for many months. Be safe, send the bylaws and eliminate the delay.

CHAPTER 16:
PART III

PROVISIONS IN YOUR ORGANIZING DOCUMENTS

"The ones who are crazy enough to think they can change the world, are the ones that do."

—Anonymous

Line 1: Location of Purpose Clause

Your organizing document must contain a purpose clause that is consistent with IRS requirements. This question wants to know exactly where it is located in your Articles of Incorporation, Articles of Association, or Declaration of Trust. Here is the example of an acceptable purpose clause contained in the IRS instructions for completing Form 1023:

"The organization is organized exclusively for charitable, religious, educational, and scientific purposes under Section 501(c) (3) of the Internal Revenue Code, or corresponding section of any future tax code."

Find that statement in your Articles of Incorporation and put the page, article, and paragraph in the blank on line 1. Don't forget to check the box to the right showing you have the required clause in your organizing document.

Line 2a: Dissolution Clause

To be approved for nonprofit status by IRS, you must have a dissolution clause that basically states that if you stop being a tax-exempt organization, all your assets will be given to another nonprofit organization. Here is an example of an acceptable dissolution clause contained in the IRS instructions for completing Form 1023:

> *"Upon the dissolution of this organization, assets will be distributed for one or more exempt purposes within the meaning of Section 501(c) (3) of the Internal Revenue Code, or corresponding section of any future federal tax code, or shall be distributed to the federal government, or to a state or local government, for a public purpose."*

Don't forget to check the box to the right showing you have the required clause in your organizing document.

Line 2b: Location of Dissolution Clause

From your organizing document, list the page, article, and paragraph of the dissolution clause.

Line 2c: Operation of State Law

If you checked 2a, you do not check this box. Most people will not use this block of the application. If you use this block, remember to check the box and fill in the state.

CHAPTER 17: PART IV

NARRATIVE DESCRIPTION OF YOUR ACTIVITIES

"If you can't explain it simply, you don't understand it well enough."

—Albert Einstein

THE HEART OF THE APPLICATION

You have come to the heart of your application and it is now time to touch the heart of the IRS agent who will be processing your package. This is your chance in a few pages, to describe the mission you are undertaking to do good things in the world. The key to getting your application approved, lies in your willingness to put forth the effort to make your vision come alive. You have to answer the questions in the IRS agent's mind, not just the ones on the application, but the other ones that any interested person would want to know when finding out about your mission.

What do you tell people about your organization when you are explaining it one-on-one or in a small group? How did your organization come into existence? What was the deciding impetus that led to its creation? What excites you most about it? Who is involved? What are their qualifications? What do you want to accomplish? How are you going to accomplish it? How will you pay for it (make sure this information agrees with your financial section of the application)? How will you select the people, groups, or organizations you will help?

Remember to answer the questions asked on the application in enough detail to answer the Who, What, When, Where, How, How Much, and Why of each question.

NO RIGHT OR WRONG WAY

There is no right or wrong way format the narrative section, but by definition, a narrative can be an essay, biographical sketch, or autobiography (in this case of the organization), usually in chronological or other logical order. Use positive, powerful terms and word choices.

Don't limit your future growth, but at the same time, do not take on the world. For example, do not say you are going to provide laptop computers to three rural schools in your state, because later you may want to provide iPads or work with schools in nearby states as well. Instead, you might say you are going to improve technology access to rural schools in your section of the U.S., beginning with providing laptop computers to three rural schools in your state. You show a small start, and give your organization room to grow in your narrative.

TELL YOUR STORY

Tell a story with your narrative and weave in the important points as part of the story. Be careful in this section not to refer to the organization with ownership; it is a separate entity that is not owned by anyone. Appendix A has many narratives that are well written. You may want to review several applications to get the flavor of this section. Live links to these online documents are available at www. doyourownnonprofit.com

Another way to get your mission across is to add copies of brochures, flyers, handouts, printed copies of website pages, and any other written material that will expand the IRS agent's understanding of what you are trying to do. You can also add short biographies of the board of directors demonstrating how they are qualified to perform the organization's mission.

You might also want to justify your procedures and structure by citing IRS regulations. You can quote specific content in the instruction booklet for filling out Form 1023, recite guidance given on the IRS website for nonprofit organizations, and quote or mention passages of IRS Revenue Rulings. You can find them online at www. irs.gov then search for Nonprofit Revenue Rulings. An example of a Revenue Ruling you might use for tax deductibility of donated items would be Revenue Ruling 2002-67. This states that:

"A donor may use an established used car pricing guide to determine the fair market value of a single donated car if the guide lists a sales price for a car that is the same make, model, and year, sold in the same area, and in the same condition, as the donated car. However, a donor may not use an established used car pricing guide to determine the fair market value of a single donated car if the guide does not list a sales price for a car in the same condition as the donated car. In such a case, the donor must use some other method that is reasonable under the circumstances to determine the value of the car. See Publication 561, "Determining the Value of Donated Property."

Your narrative might read: "Donated property to this organization will be accounted for using Publication 561 and the intent of Revenue Ruling 2002-67 which held that a donor must use methods reasonable to determine the value of the donated property."

By inserting periodic Revenue Rulings and IRS published guidance into your narrative, you give credibility to your application package and show the IRS agent that you are abreast of guidelines that affect your nonprofit operation.

NOTE: *Every page of your application and all attachments must have the organization name and EIN on it. If you are typing your narrative, you may want to include this information in a header or footer.*

CHAPTER 18:
PART V

COMPENSATION AND OTHER FINANCIAL ARRANGEMENTS WITH YOUR OFFICERS, DIRECTORS, TRUSTEES, EMPLOYEES, AND INDEPENDENT CONTRACTORS

"How wonderful it is that nobody need wait a single moment before starting to improve the world."

—Anne Frank

POSSIBLE CONFLICTS OF INTEREST

This section of your application is designed to disclose any conflicts of interest, personal profit to organization officials (or their friends, business associates, or family members), and undue influence because of relationships, contracts, and mingled loyalties between organizations. If you are a new organization with beginning operations, this section will be easy and fast to complete because chances are you will not have any of these issues to disclose.

Line 1a: List Name, Title, Mailing Address, and Compensation for All Officers, Directors, and Trustees

You can use the organization's mailing address if desired. Include exact compensation if possible. Compensation includes salary or other compensation, deferred retirement, health insurance coverage paid for by the organization, value of vehicles provided, and any other compensation in kind from use of equipment, or personal items provided such as travel or memberships. Reimbursing expenses from receipts provided is not compensation as long as the reimbursement is reasonable.

If no compensation is given, enter -0-. Information given in this section must match the financial date given in Part IX. Compensation must be reasonable for the position. Compensation that is in any way linked to income or donations to the organization waves a big red abuse flag at IRS.

Line 1b: Five Highest Compensated Employees Over $50,000 A Year That Are Not Listed In Line 1a

If you have anyone who fits this category, provide total compensation information. If not, put N/A and move on. This information must match Part IX. Compensation must be reasonable for the position.

Line 1c: Five Highest Compensated Independent Contractors Over $50,000 a Year

IRS publication 15 gives a general rule for independent contractors, which is:

> *"An individual is an independent contractor if you, the person for whom the services are performed, have the right to control or direct only the result of the work and not the means and methods of accomplishing the result."*

If you do not have anyone in that category, put N/A and move on. This information must match Part IX, Financial Data.

Line 2a: Family or Business Relationships

Here is a make-or-break question on your Form 1023. If there is a husband and wife on the board, or members that are related by blood or business, take caution. The IRS is going to look hard at your organization to make sure that related parties do not make up over half the voting power of the organization. It's best to have either husband or wife, or to add board members so that the related parties (personal or business) do not have the majority of the vote. If none, check "No." If there are relationships, check "Yes."

Explain in the narrative section answering any questions about the relationship that a reasonable person would have and eliminating the concern on the part of the IRS agent that abuse may occur as a result of this relationship.

IRS instructions list the following family relationships that need to be disclosed:

- Spouses
- Ancestors
- Children
- Grandchildren
- Great grandchildren
- Siblings (whole or half-blood)
- Spouses for any of these

Line 2b: Business Relationships with Officers, Directors, Or Trustees

Another make-or-break question on Form 1023. Other than being a part of the organization as an officer, director, or trustee, does the organization have any business relationship with these members?

For example, do you hire one of the board members to perform any services for the organization? If so, this must be disclosed. If none, check "No."

If there are relationships, check "Yes." Explain them in the narrative section answering any questions about the relationship that a reasonable person would have and eliminating the concern on the part of the IRS agent that abuse may occur as a result of this relationship.

Line 2c: Relationships Between Board Members And Highest Compensated Employees Or Independent Contractors

You guessed it – this is yet another make-or-break question. If there are any relationships between officers, directors or trustees, and your five highest compensated employees or contractors who receive over $50,000 per year, you need to disclose it here. Explain it in the narrative section answering any questions about the relationship that a reasonable person would have and eliminating the concern on the part of the IRS agent that abuse may occur as a result of this relationship.

Line 3a: Name, Qualifications, Average Hours Worked And Duties For Everyone Listed In 1a, 1b, or 1c

In the narrative section, provide this information for everyone listed even if they are volunteers who receive no compensation. If you are not sure of some of the information, give the most accurate information you can determine. If you have included a job description in your bylaws, you can simply state the page and paragraph where the job description exists for each position. If you have already listed the qualifications of the board members in the narrative, you can refer to that section instead of giving the same information again.

Line 3b: Common control

This line is designed to disclose where control rests in an organization and if there are any other organizations exercising influence and control over your organization.

Here is an example: I am on the board of directors for Kid Care America of Rolla, Inc. It is a separate organization from First Assembly of God-Rolla, but the church pays part of the salary for the director and provides facilities for the after-school program for at-risk kids. This information had to be disclosed in the Form 1023.

IRS instructions for Form 1023 define common control as:

> *"you and one or more other organizations have (1) a majority of your governing boards or officers appointed or elected by the same organization(s), or (2) a majority of your governing boards or officers consist of the same individuals. Common control also occurs when you and one or more commonly controlled organizations have a majority ownership interest (I added: more than 35%) in a corporation, partnership, or trust."*

Line 4a, 4b and 4c: Compensation-Setting Practices

"Yes" to all three of these questions means that you are using good judgment and practices in establishing compensation for your higher level officers, and also means IRS is not concerned with these items. If you answer "No" to any of these, put an explanation in the narrative.

Lines 4d, 4e, 4f, 4g: How Do You Set Reasonable Compensation And How Do You Document It?

If you arrived at your compensation by doing a comparison of other nonprofit and profit companies of similar size and function, and you document how you arrived at the compensation, then you can answer "Yes." If your board is not compensated, then you have no problems with this question. If you answer "No" to any of these questions, you must include an explanation in the narrative of how you arrived at reasonable compensation for your top officials. Overcompensating can result in loss of tax exempt status.

Lines 5a, 5b, 5c: Conflict of Interest Policy

If you have adopted a conflict of interest policy similar to the example given in Chapter 11, check "Yes" and move on. If you answered "No," you must answer lines 5b and 5c.

Lines 6a and 6b: Non-Fixed Compensation For Top Officials

If you answer "Yes" to either of these items, you have waved a huge red flag and your tax exempt status is not likely to be approved. If you are basing compensation on performance, percentages, revenue or bonuses, you are using non-fixed payments and IRS looks for corruption and sees this as a way to spread the profits around to insiders.

Lines 7a and 7b: Purchasing Goods, Services, And Assets From Top Officials, Employees, Or Contractors.

Another big red flag here if you answer "Yes." If you do purchase any goods, services, or assets from insiders, make sure you explain it well in the narrative.

Lines 8a, 8b, 8c, 8d, 8e, and 8f: Leases, Contracts, Loans, And Agreements With Insiders

Answering "Yes" to 8a does not necessarily throw up a red flag unless the compensation is more than is customary for the services or facilities in question. Remember to provide copies of all documents and include an in-depth explanation in the narrative section.

Lines 9a, 9b, 9c, 9d, 9e, and 9f: Leases, Contracts, Loans, and Agreements With Other Organizations in Which Your Officers, Directors, or Trustees Are Also Officers, Directors, or Trustees

This question looks to uncover any undue influence, or conflicts of interest, of officials who might also have influence or ownership (35% or more) in another organization you do business with. A "Yes" answer to 9a requires a thorough explanation in the narrative section and copies of any documents involved.

CHAPTER 19:
PART VI

YOUR MEMBERS AND OTHER INDIVIDUALS AND ORGANIZATIONS THAT RECEIVE BENEFITS FROM YOU

"The person who says it cannot be done should not interrupt the person who is doing it."

—Chinese Proverb

IDENTIFYING WHO WILL BENEFIT

This part of the application seeks to find out how you are selecting your target group to assist and aims to ferret out any selection process that benefits members or private interests instead of public interest. A good test is whether you know ahead of time the names of the people or organizations you will help. If so, you may not be a 501(c)(3) public charity, but a private foundation instead.

Line 1a: Benefits to Individuals

If your nonprofit organization will be helping individuals directly, check "Yes" and describe your programs and how you will carry them out. Make sure to emphasize that your target individuals are from a class of people (such as poor, disabled, homeless, or senior citizens), not specific individuals you can name ahead of time. It is permissible to help specific individuals as long as you do not limit your services to specific people, and leave opportunity to add others in the future whose name you do not even know yet. If you will be helping individuals indirectly through other organizations, check "No" and move on.

Line 1b: Benefits to Organizations

If you provide goods and services to organizations, tell what programs you will offer and how you will carry them out. Make sure to emphasize that your target organizations are from a class of organizations (such as orphanages, hospitals, schools, senior citizen homes, etc.), not specific organizations that you can name ahead of time. It is fine to begin operations helping specific organizations, but make sure your narrative reflects the desire and opportunity to add other similar organizations at a later date. If not, IRS may declare you a private foundation instead of a 501(c) (3) organization.

Line 2: Program Limits

Answering "Yes" to this item is another big red flag for IRS. If you limit your scope to specific individuals or specific organizations, you do not meet the requirement for 501(c) (3) status. You cannot select specific people or organizations ahead of time to the exclusion of all others who might be in that class or group. If you do then you are not a true public charity. For example, you cannot start a charity to benefit one specific orphanage, one specific school, or members of one specific family.

Line 3: Services to Relatives of Insiders

"Yes" to this question is another red flag to IRS. If the answer is "Yes," you must disclose it. Give a detailed explanation in the narrative.

CHAPTER 20:
PART VII

YOUR HISTORY

"Our lives begin to end the day we become silent about things that matter."

—Martin Luther King, Jr.

This section tells whether your organization was formed from a previous organization, and whether you have filed for 501(c) (3) status within 27 months of filing your Articles of Incorporation.

Line 1: Are You a "Successor" To Another Organization?

If you answer "Yes," it means that you have taken over all the assets or activities of another organization, been converted or merged from another organization, and/or have the same officials as another organization that doesn't exist anymore but served the same function. The previous organization could have been a tax exempt organization, but does not have to be.

An example that comes to mind is in my town. Twenty or so years ago, there was an organization called LOVE (Local Organization of Various Enterprises), that assisted people who had difficulty paying utility bills in winter, buying food, and paying rent. LOVE was closed, and the organization was converted to another organization called

GRACE (Greater Rolla Area Charitable Enterprises). It has become a one-stop facility for anyone who needs help with living expenses.

Local churches and helping organizations send everyone to GRACE first, and records are kept there of who received what help from where, and when they received it. This has stopped abuse of people taking advantage of the helping organizations in this area.

United Way lets residents contribute to GRACE, and local schools have canned food drives at holidays to assist GRACE in its mission. So GRACE was the successor of LOVE, and in this case, both were nonprofit tax exempt organizations.

If you answer "Yes," you must complete Schedule G of the application.

Line 2: Time Limit of 27 Months to File For Tax-Exempt Status

IRS gives you 27 months to file Form 1023 from the last day of the month in which your organization was formed, or your Articles of Incorporation were filed with the state. If you file within that time, your tax exempt status can be effective from day one. If you miss the 27 month deadline, your application can be approved, but will only be effective from the date of the postmark on the application. This could cause a problem for your donors because their donations would not be deductible before the postmarked date. You can request a waiver but there is no guarantee you will get it.

If you did not file within 27 months, you will need to fill out and attach Schedule E to the application. You might be eligible for 501(c)(4) status for the time that does not qualify for 501(c) (3) status, but that requires you to file a Form 1024 in addition to this Form 1023. Best and easiest to file within the 27 month window.

CHAPTER 21:
PART VIII

SPECIFIC ACTIVITIES

"If you do what you've always done, you'll get what you've always gotten."

—Tony Robbins

Line 1: Do You Support or Oppose Candidates In Political Campaigns In Any Way?

If you answer this question "Yes," you just wasted a lot of time and effort, because 501(c) (3) organizations CANNOT engage in political activities that endorse or oppose candidates. Period. End of Conversation. NO EXCEPTIONS.

Involving yourself in any political activity can be hazardous to your tax exempt status. Because rightly dividing the regulations can be tricky, it is best to call IRS and discuss any proposed activities with them before you engage in them so as not to jeopardize 501(c) (3) status eligibility.

Line 2a: Do you attempt to influence legislation?

This is yet another fine line to navigate. If you answer "Yes," that means you are trying to persuade people to support or oppose legislation. You must give an explanation in the narrative that spells out how much time and money you are spending on it. Tax exempt organizations are not allowed to engage in "substantial legislative activities." Although "substantial" is not well defined, case law has shown over time that 5% of time and money is NOT substantial, while 16% is.

This is a tricky area. If you answer "Yes," you may want to contact a professional to assist you with meeting the requirements of the Internal Revenue Code and applicable Treasury regulations. Failure to abide within the parameters can result in loss of tax exempt status, not getting tax exempt status in the first place, and excise taxes being levied against the organization.

Line 2b: Form 5768, Election/Revocation of Election by an Eligible Section 501(c)(3) Organization To Make Expenditures To Influence Legislation

If you answered "Yes" to line 2a, you may elect to have your activities to influence legislation calculated by how much you spent based on Section 501(h). See Publication 557 for more details on filing Form 5768. Churches and private foundations are not allowed to complete Form 5768. Do yourself a favor and call IRS if you have any dealings in this area.

Lines 3a, 3b, and 3c: Bingo

If you are going to conduct Bingo games or have them conducted on your behalf, answer these questions to fit your plans and circumstances. Provide details in the narrative. Remember that winners of high stakes Bingo games must be reported to IRS so they can collect the taxes due on the winnings. If you are not going to engage in Bingo in any facet, mark "No," and move on.

Lines 4a, 4b, 4c, 4d, and 4e: Fundraising

Whatever you put here must be explained, described, and it's a good idea to include copies of any paperwork you use. If you are contemplating a certain type of fundraising but have not firmed up specifics or undertaken that mode of fundraising yet, you might want to leave it off for now. Put only what you are actually doing or will actually do in the near term.

The more you include, the more justification and paperwork you need, and the more chance that something will be questioned. I do not advocate leaving out anything material. Be honest and complete, but leave your future plans to the future, especially if you have not ironed out enough details to pass IRS scrutiny at the time of this application. Make sure this line agrees with Part IX, Financial Data.

You should be aware that IRS will look hard at any applicant who plans to use professional fundraiser. This is an area of frequent abuse of donor-advised accounts for personal gain, so IRS is skeptical, and you may be subject to excise tax or not be granted 501(c) (3) status. Contact IRS to discuss your specific situation.

You might want to review some of the Form 1023 links in Appendix A to see how other organizations have addressed fundraising on the application and in the narrative. You do not need to reinvent the wheel.

Line 5: Government Unit Affiliation

Government units are not normally eligible for 501(c) (3) status because they have power to establish, control, manage, and/or supervise legal or government issues. However, some organizations, such as municipal hospitals, are affiliated with government units or Indian Tribal Governments, and are eligible because they do not have those powers, or because they lessen the burden on the government. If you answer "Yes," include an explanation in the narrative. If not, check "No" and move on.

Lines 6a and 6b: Economic Development

Organizations created to counter deterioration of neighborhoods that have been recognized by a government agency as economically depressed, deteriorating, or blighted, qualify for 501(c) (3) status as economic development organizations. The services provided can be loans, grants, sharing knowledge and skill with business plans or other business development tasks. Services can also include creation of industrial parks as well as to aid in eliminating prejudice and discrimination, or to decrease government burdens through business development.

IRS instructions for completing Line 6a include the following guidance:

> "If your exempt purpose is to combat community deterioration, describe whether the area or areas in which you will operate have been declared blighted or economically depressed by a government finding. If the area has not been declared blighted or economically depressed, a more suitable exemption may be under Sections 501(c) (4) or 501(c)(6). See Publication 557 for more information.
>
> If your exempt purpose is to eliminate prejudice and discrimination, describe how your activities further this purpose.
>
> If your exempt purpose is to lessen the burdens of government, describe whether the government has recognized your activities as those for which it would otherwise be responsible, and any involvement you have with governmental entities that demonstrates that you are actually lessening governmental burdens."

For Line 6b, in the narrative, include a complete description of your target audience and how your services will fulfill exempt purposes.

Lines 7a, 7b, and 7c: Development and Management Relationships

Once again IRS is looking for abuse or situations in which insiders and their families, friends, and business associates unfairly benefit or profit from affiliation with a tax exempt organization. If any of these apply, full disclosure is required in terms of explanation, description of services, and copies of all agreements and contracts. You must explain how compensation was arrived at and how you ensured it was reasonable for services rendered or to be completed. Expect IRS scrutiny if you answer "Yes" to these.

Line 8: Joint Ventures

This item seeks to establish whether your tax exempt organization plans to join forces with other individuals or organizations that are not 501(c) (3) approved, for profit purposes. IRS instructions for this line define a joint venture as:

> *"A legal agreement in which the persons jointly undertake a transaction for mutual profit. Generally, each person contributes assets and shares risks. Like a partnership, a joint venture can involve any kind of business transaction and the persons involved can be individuals, companies, or corporations."*

A nonprofit that I founded (Pasture Valley Children Missions, EIN 35-2468924) entered a joint venture with a local pharmacy to provide a market for jewelry made by orphans in Swaziland. The agreement called for a 20% commission (the pharmacy's standard commission) on all items sold. This is the type of agreement that would need to be disclosed and explained if known or planned at the time of application. As it turned out, no commission was actually ever charged. The pharmacy donated the commission to the organization instead.

The same type of agreement was made with another organization to market the jewelry, but no disclosure was required because the second organization was also a tax exempt organization.

This is a tricky area, and I highly recommend you talk with IRS about it if you have any joint ventures in force or planned with organizations that are not tax exempt.

Lines 9a, 9b, 9c, and 9d: Childcare Organizations

Two choices exist for tax exempt status here. You can be tax exempt as a childcare facility if you are classified as a school under Internal Revenue Code 170(b)(1)(A)(ii) which reads:

> *"An educational organization which normally maintains a regular faculty and curriculum and normally has a regularly enrolled body of pupils or students in attendance at the place where its educational activities are regularly carried on."*

You must complete Schedule B of the application in addition to the Form 1023.

The second choice is a 501(k) childcare organization. You can qualify under Section 501(k) if the kids come to your location, you are allowing parents to work or seek work, and you serve the general public. If you are only serving a specific employer or group, you are not eligible for 501(c) (3) status. At least 85% of those families you serve must meet these conditions, or you must describe how you are going to meet the requirement and increase the percentage to 85% to be eligible for tax exempt status.

Line 10: Intellectual Property

IRS instructions say that intellectual property includes patents for inventions; copyrights (for literary and artistic works such as novels, poems, plays, films, musical works, drawings, paintings, photographs, sculptures, architectural designs, performances, recordings, film, and radio or television programs); trade names, trademarks, and service marks (for symbols, names, images, and designs); and formulas, know-how, and trade secrets.

Intellectual property also includes any written materials either published, printed, copied, or displayed on a website online. If you have a slogan or a logo, this is also intellectual property. If you are just starting out and have none of these yet, answer "No."

If you have developed any educational materials, brochures, or websites or any intellectual property from the ones listed above, you must answer "Yes," and give complete details on all items required for this line.

Line 11: Contributions of Real Property

Although cash is real, real property is anything but cash. IRS is concerned about scams and abuse in this area. The main areas of concern are how some are overvaluing the property for tax deduction purposes, and who has actual control of the contributed item.

Lines 12a, 12b, and 12c: Operating in Foreign Countries

If you have operations in foreign countries, you need to explain the locations, operations, and how those operations promote or advance your tax exempt purpose. It is allowed and you can quote revenue rulings in your narrative as support for your foreign operations.

Although tax deductions are not permitted for giving to foreign charities, people and businesses can donate to a U.S. 501(c) (3) approved organization that gives to foreign charities or support foreign charitable causest. Since 911, funneling money into terrorist activities has been a concern. You may want to explicitly state that your organization has no ties to terrorist activities and that all foreign operations are for tax exempt purposes within the letter and the intent of Section 501(c) (3) of the Internal Revenue Code.

Line 13a, 13b, 13c, 13d, 13e, 13f, and 13g: Distributions to Organizations

If you make grants, loans, or distributions to organizations, you need to answer each part of this section and include copies of all forms you use in deciding who is eligible for a distribution, how much they get, and how you will monitor the funds to make sure they are being used for exempt purposes.

You also need to describe how you will keep records and reports you will require. If there is a relationship between you and the grantee, you must disclose the details in your narrative.

Here is an acceptable way to answer Line 13e (you can borrow these words if they apply):

(Organization) will maintain its financial records on QuickBooks software in accordance with general accounting principles for non-profit organizations. Cash received is applied to Accounts Receivable Ledger and cash distributed is recorded in the Accounts Payable Ledger. Likewise, organizations that receive distributions are required to maintain general accounting records, and are required to report on a regular/monthly basis as to how, when and where funds are applied.

Lines 14a, 14b, 14c, 14d, 14e, and 14f: Distributions to foreign organizations

If you distribute funds to foreign organizations, you must explain to IRS how you make sure the money is going for its tax exempt purpose. As you answer the questions in this section, you may want to include a statement in the narrative that states if the organizations you are distributing to were located in the United States, they would qualify for 501(c) (3) status because their purposes are consistent with Section 501(c) (3).

Line 15: Do You Have a Close Connection to Any Other Organization?

Another item designed to detect undue influence or abuse. IRS instructions for this item specify that a close connection exists if:

You control the organization or it controls you through common officers, directors, or trustees, or through authority to approve budgets or expenditures. You and the organization were created at approximately the same time and by the same persons. For example, you were formed within months of the time that a social welfare organization and a political action committee were established by the same persons who were instrumental in your formation.

You and the organization operate in a coordinated manner with respect to facilities, programs, employees, or other activities. For example, you share rental expenses for office space and employees with a for-profit corporation.

Persons who exercise substantial influence over you also exercise substantial influence over the other organization and (1) you either conduct activities in common or (2) have a financial relationship. For example, a voting member of your governing body is also a voting member of the governing body of a business league with which you intend to cooperate in planning an advertising campaign that will inform the public about the benefits of a particular program. For example, a voting member of your governing body is also a voting member of the governing body of a business league that has made a loan to you.

A tax exempt organization (such as Kid Care America of Rolla, Inc.) can have a close connection to another tax exempt organization (such as First Assembly of God-Rolla), and this is not an issue. Both are 501(c) (3) approved, so it is fine for them to share facilities, have some of the same people involved in both organizations, and share some expenses of conducting tax exempt activities.

Line 16: Cooperative Hospital Service Organizations

Section 501(e) lists operations that fall under the heading of cooperative hospital service organizations. They include: data processing, purchasing, warehousing, billing and collection, food, clinical, industrial engineering, laboratory, printing, communications, record center, and personnel services. Only a narrow percentage of 501(e) organizations can make the cut to get 501(c) (3) status. If you answered "Yes" to this item, call IRS and discuss the specifics before submitting your application.

Line 17: Cooperative Service Organizations of Operating Educational Organizations

These organizations perform collective investment services for educational organizations. IRS Publication 557 advises that if you answer "Yes" to this item, call IRS and discuss the specifics of your eligibility for 501(c) (3) status because this type of organization falls under Section 501(f) but the Form 1023 is still used to apply.

Line 18: Charitable Risk Pool

This type of organization provides insurance. If that describes you, contact IRS and discuss the details to determine if you are eligible for tax exempt status. IRS lists the following criteria for exemption:

A charitable risk pool is treated as organized and operated exclusively for charitable purposes if it:

1. Is organized and operated only to pool insurable risks of its members (not including risks related to medical malpractice) and to provide information to its members about loss control and risk management,
2. Consists only of members that are Section 501(c) (3) organizations exempt from tax under Section 501(a)
3. Is organized under state law authorizing this type of risk pooling,
4. Is exempt from state income tax (or will be after qualifying as a Section 501(c) (3) organization),
5. Has obtained at least $1,000,000 in startup capital from nonmember charitable organizations,
6. Is controlled by a board of directors elected by its members, and
7. Is organized under documents requiring that:

a. Each member be a Section 501(c) (3) organization exempt from tax under Section 501(a)

b. Each member that receives a final determination that it no longer qualified under Section 501(c) (3) notify the pool immediately, and

c. Each insurance policy issued by the pool provide that it will not cover events occurring after a final determination described in (b).

Line 19: Do You or Will You Operate a School?

You have extra paperwork to submit if you are applying for 501(c) (3) status as a school, as well as proving you have a well-publicized nondiscrimination policy. IRS defines a school as:

> *"An educational organization whose primary function is the presentation of formal instruction and which normally maintains a regular faculty and curriculum and normally has a regularly enrolled body of pupils or students in attendance at the place where its educational activities are regularly carried on."*

This may include any level of compulsory education as well as higher education, trade and technical schools, and preschools or nurseries. In addition, schools that are part of museums, historical societies, or churches are also eligible. You will have to fill out Schedule B with your application. For specifics, do an internet search for IRS Publication 557 and read beginning on page 27.

Line 20: Hospital or Medical Care

This type of organization treats medical conditions, including mental disability, either on an inpatient or outpatient basis. IRS recognizes rehab, mental health, and drug treatment centers; and medical education and research facilities as part of this category. You must complete Schedule C as part of your application. There are many rules for this category and I suggest you call IRS and discuss the specifics before filing Form 1023. In addition, read new guidelines found at www.irs.gov then search for New Requirements for 501(c)(3) Hospitals under the Affordable Care Act.

Line 21: Elderly or Handicapped and Low Income Housing

IRS instructions give the following definitions and guidance:

- "Low-income housing" refers to rental or ownership housing provided to persons based on financial need.
- "Elderly housing" refers to rental or ownership housing provided to persons based on age, including retirement, assisted-living, independent living, continuous care, and life care arrangements.
- "Handicapped housing" refers to rental or ownership housing provided to persons based on physical or mental disabilities, including nursing homes. If you are a skilled nursing facility, you should also complete *Schedule C*.

This category has many rules to comply with, so I suggest you contact IRS and discuss your specifics before filing. You must also file Schedule F with your application.

Line 22: Scholarships, Fellowships, Loans, and Grants

IRS instructions for this line include the following guidance:

- Answer "Yes" if you pay monies to an individual as a scholarship, fellowship, or educational loan, for travel, study, or other similar purposes. Also answer "Yes" if you pay such amounts on behalf of an individual to a school or a tuition or educational savings program.
- Travel, study, or other similar purposes include payments made to enhance a literary, artistic, musical, scientific, teaching or

other similar capacity, skill, or talent of the individual recipient. For example amounts paid to:

- Vocational high school students to be used to purchase basic tools.
- Teachers to induce them to teach in an economically depressed, public school system.
- A scientific researcher to underwrite that individual's research project.

Educational grants do not include amounts you pay to an individual as compensation, such as payments made to a consultant for personal services or to produce a report for you.

Educational grants do not include amounts paid to another organization that distributes your funds as a scholarship to an individual if you have no role in the selection process.

IRS will want a copy of your scholarship application with the Form 1023, and a completed Schedule H.

CHAPTER 22:
PART IX

FINANCIAL DATA

*"The question isn't who is going to let me; it's who
is going to stop me."*

—Ayn Rand

LOOKING AT THE FINANCES

This section may seem difficult or tricky, but it does not have to be. IRS wants to know what has occurred financially to date with your organization, and/or what you expect to happen in the near future (the next few years). If you are a brand new organization that has had nothing but minimal financial support or transactions, then this part is very easy to complete. Just remember that what you put in this section has to match the rest of the application including the narrative. Also be aware that IRS issued an update (Notice 1382) requiring financial information for three years if you are less than one year old, and four years if you are more than one year old).

Bear in mind that the application filing fee is based on the actual (for organizations that have been around for a while) or projected (for new organizations just getting started) income of the organization.

If the average combined gross revenue over a four year period of time is less than $10,000 per year, the filing fee is currently $400. If it is over $10,000 a year, the fee is $850. The application says $300 and $750 because IRS did not reprint the form, they simply issued an update stating the price had gone up. If you do not know what your revenues will be, give it your best educated guess. IRS will not penalize you if you guess too low, or refund you if you guess too high. You are projecting, so just do the best you can. A projection is a guess, a prediction, an estimate.

If you are using a standard financial software program like QuickBooks, you can print the required reports and attach them instead of filling out the forms in Part IX. Simply write "See Attached" and place the reports behind the appropriate page of the application so that the IRS agent won't have to look for it. The easier you make it, the less time and correspondence will be required to get your determination letter.

You will need a statement of revenue and expenses (either actual, projected, or a combination of the two), and a balance sheet. That's it. Don't let the columns and categories overwhelm you. It's possible that much of it doesn't even apply to your organization. If a line doesn't apply to you, leave it blank or put in a zero and move on.

HINT: Start by putting zeroes on all the lines in all the columns that do not apply. That way you can see progress immediately and only have to deal with the blanks that do not have zeroes. This can make the task seem easier and less complicated.

October 2013 Revision (Notice 1382) defines "Years in existence" as completed tax years. Instructions below incorporate these October 2013 changes, although they will not be on the actual forms until IRS publishes a revised form.

If you have been in existence for five or more years, chances are you already have financial statements for that timeframe. IRS wants to see them for the past five years or as long as you have been in business if it is less than five years. Attach them on the *Revenue and Expenses* form, include the current year and the previous up to three years financial data, and attach projected financial data to cover five years total (actual and projected). Complete the balance sheet for the previous tax year and remember to end it on the last day of the last month of the last full tax year. For example, if your tax year ends

December 31, then the balance sheet would have an ending date of December 31 last year.

If you have been in existence for one, but less than four years, attach your own revenue and expense statements. Or use the first column to provide revenue and expenses for this year to date (actually as of the last day of last month). Use the other columns for years you have existed prior to this year, and any leftover columns to project your income and expenses to the best of your ability for future years. This way you are providing four full years of either actual or projected income, plus information for this year to date. Be sure to put correct dates in the columns so that IRS knows what is actual and what is projected. Mark any attached financial statements clearly so there is no misinterpretation of whether you are giving past historical financial data, or projections of what you expect to happen. Remember, if you have completed one full tax year, IRS wants to see up to four years of financial statements, depending on how long you have been operating.

If you have been in existence less than one year, this is going to be so easy! You get to make the whole thing up for three years, giving it your best effort to determine the most likely income and expenses. So what if you don't know for sure? Give it your best shot. Start somewhere, and think it through. Don't stress out over it. Just do it! No penalty for being wrong, but be as accurate as you can, knowing full well you won't know the real numbers until after the fact. IRS knows it is not accurate, you know it is not accurate, but they make you do it anyway. So just do it.

You can do this, it is just paperwork, one line at a time, so let's get started:

Line 1: Gifts, Grants, and Contributions Received (do not include unusual gifts)

Unusual grants are unexpected large sums received from a disinterested party. Because the amount is large, it can affect your organization's classification as a public charity which must be supported primarily by the general public. For this reason, grants like this are reported further down on the form on Line 12.

On line 1, you report gifts, grants, and contributions from various sources that help you accomplish your tax exempt purpose. You also report government units helping you that provide a service or facility to the general public (as opposed to a specific group). If you receive revenue to complete a program or function for the general public (for example, hired by someone or an organization), report it on this line. If you sell tickets to the general public as opposed to being hired for a fee to perform, that income goes on Line 9, Gross Receipts. If you are not sure which line to put the income on, contact IRS and ask before filling out the form.

Line 2: Membership Fees

Most charitable nonprofits do not have membership fees because they do not have members. If you do have members and you charge a membership fee to support the organization, put the total of the fees on this line. Do not include fees charged to members for anything except membership. Any other fees paid (such as for admission, merchandise, services, or use of facilities) is gross receipts, not membership fees.

Line 3: Gross Investment Income

Any income received from any investment (loans, rents, royalties, dividends, interest, etc.) is entered here.

Line 4: Net Unrelated Business Income

Do you have any income from unrelated business activity? Any income of which less than 85% of the labor was not completed by volunteers? Any income that did not have anything to do with your exempt purpose? You report it on line 4. Contact IRS or see Publication 598 if you need more information on this line, specifically Chapter 4 to figure the unrelated business income. You can access it at www.irs.gov then searching for Publication 598.

Line 5: Taxes Levied For Your Benefit

If the public paid any taxes on your behalf, include the amount collected here.

Line 6: Value of Services or Facilities Furnished by a Government Unit without Charge (not including the value of services generally furnished to the public without charge)

Use the fair market value that would be charged for an organization that is not tax exempt.

Line 7: Any Revenue Not Otherwise Listed Above or on Lines 9–12 below.

(Attach an itemized list) In my opinion, this line should have come AFTER line 12 because you have to complete lines 9–12 before you can answer this one. If you have other forms of income that do not fit into one of the other categories, put them here. Itemize them, and give a brief description (less brief if you think IRS needs more details to avoid sending you a letter asking for more information). If in doubt, contact IRS and ask before entering it here.

Line 8: Total lines 1 – 7

Use a calculator and add every column, as well as a total of all columns in the far right column.

Line 9: Gross Receipts from Admissions, Merchandise Sold, or Services Performed, or Furnishing of Facilities in Any Activity that is Related to Your Exempt Purposes

(Attach itemized list) Do not include amounts you have already included on other lines of this form. You only want to count the amounts once. If you received funds for use of facilities that was not for the direct benefit of the general public, list it here. You must itemize and include what government agency paid you, purpose of the payment, and the amount. If in doubt, contact IRS and see Publication 598 before filling out this line.

Line 10: Total of lines 8 and 9

Enter the total of both lines in each column and combine the totals in the far right column.

Line 11: Net Gain or Loss on the Sale of Capital Assets

(Attach schedule and see instructions) This is the format for the schedule referred to in this question (from the IRS website):

FIGURE 2. PART IX-A. STATEMENT OF REVENUES AND EXPENSES LINE 11. NET GAIN OR (LOSS)

		Categories		
		(A) Real Estate	**(B) Securities**	**(C) Other**
1.	Gross sales price of assets (other than inventory) by category.			
2.	**Less:** Cost or other basis and sales expenses.			
3.	Gain or (loss). Subtract line 2 from line 1.			
4.	Net gain or (loss)–Add line 3 of columns (A), (B), and (C). Enter here and on Form 1023, Part IX–A. Statement of Revenues and Expenses, line 11.			

If this line applies to your organization, put the total amounts for each category (not an itemized list). Create this format as best you can to include all required information, as an actual form does not exist.

Line 12: Unusual Grants

Did you unexpectedly receive a large grant from a disinterested party? This is where you record it. You must also completely describe your unusual grant in Part X, line 7. More information is available in Publication 557 available at www.irs.gov

Line 13: Total Revenue. (Add lines 10-12)

Add each column, put in the total, and also the cumulative total in the far right column.

Line 14: Fundraising Expenses

What are you spending (or plan to spend) for fundraising? If you hire a professional fundraiser, you must disclose the amount paid here as well. IRS scrutinizes hiring professional fundraisers. The income for fundraising should be on line 1, and this line has to do with any expenses incurred to make the fundraising revenue reported on line 1.

Line 15: Contributions, Gifts, Grants, And Similar Amounts Paid Out

(Attach itemized list). Who received it? How much? What for? If disclosing the name of the individual receiving the payout violates privacy provisions (such as names of those who receive scholarships), then lump the totals together and list them by program or category instead of by person.

Line 16: Disbursements To Or For The Benefit Of Members

(Attach an itemized list) If you disbursed funds to members of your organization, full disclosure of who, how much, and why is required. IRS instructions for this form say not to include any amount already included in line 15. Make sure to explain this item completely. Exempt organizations under Section 501(c) (3) exist to benefit the public, not their members, so this area can be a little tricky. If in doubt, contact IRS and talk with them about your specifics before filling out this line.

Line 17: Compensation of Officers, Directors, and Trustees

In Part V of the application, you were asked to list the officers, directors, and trustees and their compensation. Make sure the information provided here matches the information given there. Enter the totals for all columns.

Line 18: Other Salary and Wages

Do you have any employees who are not officers, directors, and trustees? Enter the totals paid to them in all columns.

Line 19: Interest Expense

How much interest did you pay, if any? Do not include mortgage interest if it is being reported as part of an occupancy expense on line 20.

Line 20: Occupancy

Utilities, mortgage interest, real estate taxes, janitorial services, rent, electricity, heat, etc. This includes all facilities for which you pay these expenses to complete your exempt purpose. Enter the total for all columns.

Line 21: Depreciation and Depletion

These are calculated the same way they would be in a for-profit organization, the same rules apply. If in doubt, contact IRS and ask before filling in this line.

Line 22: Professional Fees

Accounting, consulting, legal counsel, contract management, and other fees paid to people or organizations who are not your employees. Do not include professional fundraising fees here that you have already reported on line 14. Independent contractor fees would be reported on this line.

Line 23: Any Expense Not Otherwise Classified, Such As Program Services

(Attach itemized list) If you have expenses you have not included above, combine the totals here and make an itemized list. Examples of expenses that may not be included above could be the filing fee for your tax exempt application, the cost of this book, postage, telephone service (if not included in occupancy above), vehicle expenses, insurance payments, website fees, even bank charges can be included here. This is the catch-all line very much like the one at the end of Schedule C of Form 1040 for business owners.

Line 24: Total Expenses. (Add Lines 14 -23)

Total the expenses in all columns.

BALANCE SHEET

A balance sheet is a financial statement that ascertains the net worth of a business on a specific date. It includes the assets and the liabilities. If your financial software has a balance sheet program, you can print it and attach it behind this section. Just be sure to write "See Attached" on this section of application. If not, use the form in the application.

IRS wants to know the net worth as of the last day of the most recently completed tax year. If your tax year ends in December, then the date would be December 31 of last year. This is great news for a new nonprofit that did not exist on December 31 last year. Every line gets a zero and you are ready to move on.

If your organization did exist as of the last day of your most recent tax year, then the information you provide should reflect the status as of that date.

ASSETS

Line 1: Cash

Combine all short term assets (less than one year until maturity) and put the total in. This includes, cash, petty cash, money in checking and savings accounts, money markets, certificates of deposit, treasury bills, etc.

Line 2: Accounts Receivable, Net

Unpaid accounts that you expect to collect from sales or services, minus any reserve for bad debts.

Line 3: Inventories

What do you have on hand that you bought, or made, and are either going to use or sell in the future? What is the inventory worth after you subtract the cost to produce or acquire it?

Line 4. Bonds and Notes Receivable

(Attach an itemized list) This item is for bonds or notes your organization issued that you expect to be repaid to you. The itemized list needs to include the borrower's name, what the form of the obligation is and a description, the rate of return, when it is due and how much is due.

Line 5: Corporate Stocks

(Attach an itemized list) What is the fair market value of stocks your organization holds? The itemized list should include any stocks from closely-held corporations (those companies in which although the public owns some stock, most of it is held by a few people who have no plans to sell it). Include the name of the company, its capital structure, how many shares are held, and the fair market value. For stock listed on an exchange or sold in sufficient quantities Over the Counter (OTC stock) to make it liquid, you must include the name of the company, the exchange, identify the stock and number of shares, and the fair market value.

Line 6: Loans Receivable

(Attach an itemized list) If your organization made loans, either uncollateralized or mortgage loans, you must list each loan separately and who the loans were made to, the amount, the purpose, what interest rate, and terms for how the loan is being paid back. Total all the loans and put that amount on line 6.

Line 7: Other Investments

(Attach an itemized list) This is where you list items, government securities, or properties held for investment. List them separately on an attached sheet and give the value of each.

Line 8: Depreciable and Depletable Assets

(Attach an itemized list) This is where you list items, equipment, or buildings not held for investment. Be sure to include the cost basis of the item in the itemized list. The cost basis is the original cost minus depreciation.

Line 9: Land

This is where you list land that the organization owns that is not for investment.

Line 10: Other Assets

(Attach an itemized list) Anything else the organization owns, including patents and intellectual property gets a book value assigned and is listed here.

Line 11: Total Assets (Add lines 1 through 10)

Add them all up and put in the total.

LIABILITIES

Line 12: Accounts Payable

Include bills that need to be paid or are payable but not yet due. For example, suppliers, salaries, accumulated payroll taxes, and interest.

Line 13: Contributions, Gifts, Grants, Etc. Payable

What commitments have you made that you have not yet paid for? For example, are you obligated to a scholarship but have not written the check? This category includes individuals and organizations you have made commitments to.

Line 14: Mortgages and Notes Payable

(Attach an itemized list) What is the balance due for notes and mortgages at the end of the current tax year/period? On the itemized list, show each note or mortgage, the lender, purpose, repayment terms, interest rate, and the original amount of the loan.

Line 15: Other Liabilities

(Attach an itemized list) If you owe anything else, put it here and list it on the attachment with enough details to satisfy the IRS agent's curiosity.

Line 16: Total Liabilities

(Add lines 12 through 15). Put the total in on this line.

FUND BALANCES OR NET ASSETS

Line 17: Total Fund Balances or Net Assets

Assets minus liabilities equals fund balances and may also be called net assets. For purposes here, if your software program uses fund accounting, report it. Otherwise, use only net assets which include capital stock, paid-in capital, retained earnings or accumulated income, and endowment funds.

Line 18: Total Liabilities and Fund Balances or Net Assets (Add lines 16 and 17)

Put the total on this line.

Line 19: Have There Been Any Substantial Changes In Assets or Liabilities Since The End of The Period Shown Above?

If "Yes," explain. Don't forget to explain why the change occurred.

CHAPTER 23:
PART X

PUBLIC CHARITY STATUS

"If you can dream it, you can achieve it."

—Zig Ziglar

WHY YOU ARE A PUBLIC CHARITY

Part X is where you establish yourself as a public charity, which is eligible for 501(c) (3), instead of a private foundation. If it is the latter, donations may not be completely deductible (often limited to 30%–50%). If you are a private foundation, I suggest you consult IRS about your requirements.

In the beginning of this book, we looked at why you would be a public charity instead of a private foundation. In brief, your source of income in a private foundation does not come from the public, while a public charity's revenues do. To be a public charity, you must be a church, school, hospital, government unit, be testing for public safety, receive most of your support from the general public, or support other organizations that are public charities. Otherwise, you are a private foundation.

Line 1a: Are You a Private Foundation?

If you can answer "No" because you are a public charity, go to Line 5. A private foundation is one in which most of the support comes from predetermined sources such as a specific company or family. Private foundations pay some taxes on their investment income and cannot do as they want or invest where they want to. There are some restrictions that affect their operation.

Line 1b: Mandatory Provisions

If you answer "Yes," to Line 1a, your organizing documents must contain the required language for tax exempt eligibility, and you must include an explanation giving the location of these provisions in your documents. The suggested wording is contained in chapter 7 of this book. Well over half the states require the mandatory provisions be included in the foundation's governing instruments.

Line 2: Direct Involvement for the Active Conduct of Tax Exempt Purposes

If your foundation actually runs its own programs instead of contributes money to other organizations running tax exempt programs, then you check "Yes," and continue the application. If "No," sign the application at the end of Part XI.

Line 3: Have You Existed For One Or More Years?

If "Yes," attach financial statements and sign Part XI. If no, continue.

Line 4: Attachments

If you have been around for less than a year, then you need proof or at least verification from an attorney of what your operations are and how you will fund them, and that they satisfy the requirements to be categorized as a private foundation. If you do not have opinion of counsel, you can provide a statement giving the required information.

Line 5: Type of Public Charity.

Somewhere in the list for line 5, you will find the type that fits your charity. If unsure, contact IRS and ask them to help you decide. Many organizations select 5g because they rely on the public for much of their support and they do not fall into some other category such as a church, school, a hospital, or exist to support another tax exempt organization.

If you select 5a, 5b, 5c, or 5d, you have an additional schedule to complete. Instructions for these schedules are contained in the next chapter.

If you select 5e, 5f, 5g, 5h, or 5i, you do not have any additional schedules to complete. You can select 5i and let IRS decide what type of public charity you are. This will delay approval of tax exempt status if they determine you are one of the categories that need to fill out an additional schedule. Call them instead.

For public charity status, there is a one-third public support test you must meet or a 10% facts and circumstance test. It's not that complicated. If at least one third of your support comes from the public, you can have public charity status. If between 10% and 33% comes from the public, but there are circumstances to be considered, then you may qualify under the facts and circumstances test.

Line 6a: Advanced Ruling

This section no longer applies and should not be filled out. DO NOT SIGN IT. IRS did not reprint the form to eliminate it, they simply issued an update (Notice 1382) saying not to fill it out anymore.

Line 6b: Definitive Ruling

If you are less than five years old, you get a pass on this question as well. Notice 1382 says not to complete it unless your organization is at least five years old.

If you are more than five years old, you have already completed the financial data so that you can answer the questions in Line 6b.

Line 7: Unusual grants

Once again, Notice 1382 made this line to only apply to organizations that have been operating for five or more years.

CHAPTER 24:
PART X

SCHEDULES A, B, C, D

"You must be the change you want to see in the world."
—Mahatma Gandhi

SCHEDULE A: CHURCHES

If it looks like a church, acts like a church, and functions like a church, it is probably a church. This classification includes mosques, temples, synagogues, etc. There must be a congregation or other membership.

IRS has some specific attributes it wants to know about. You do not need to have them all, but if some are missing that are typical for a church, or if the congregation is very small, it may create some thought of fraud or misrepresentation in the IRS agent's mind. Here is the list of attributes according to IRS:

- A distinct legal existence.
- A recognized creed and form of worship.
- A definite and distinct ecclesiastical government.
- A formal code of doctrine and discipline.
- A distinct religious history.

- A membership not associated with any other church or denomination.
- Ordained ministers ministering to the congregation.
- Ordained ministers selected after completing prescribed courses of study.
- A literature of its own.
- Established places of worship.
- Regular congregations.
- Regular religious services.
- Sunday schools for the religious instruction of the young.
- Schools for the preparation of ministers.

Line 1a: Written Statement of Faith

Your written creed, statement of faith, or summary of beliefs must be attached.

Line 1b: Form of Worship

What are the practices of your church that show your dedication to your beliefs?

Line 2a: Code of Doctrine and Discipline

What laws or rules do you function under?

Line 2b: Religious History

Give an overview of how you came into being, tell your history and milestones.

Line 2c: Literature

Any writings containing any of the above items: practices, rules, laws, doctrines, history.

Line 3: Religious Hierarchy or Ecclesiastical Government

What is the chain of command?

Line 4a: Regularly Scheduled Religious Services

Give days of the week and times, order of events, and an explanation of how these activities further your religious purpose. Include copies of church bulletins, pamphlets, or other printed material handed out to members or the public.

Line 4b: Average Attendance

If the congregation numbers are small, IRS is suspicious.

Line 5a and 5b: Established Place Of Worship And Ownership

You do not need to own the location which you use to conduct services. You can rent it or it can be provided to you for no charge. If you do not have a location, where are you meeting?

Line 6: Established Congregation

This means an established membership that includes people from more than one family. If you do not have an established membership yet, you can wait to file the application until you do, or choose another public charity type on Part X, Line 5 of Form 1023. If in doubt, contact IRS and discuss your circumstances. Very small congregations are suspect to IRS.

Line 7: Number of Members

Enter number of members or if none, enter zero.

Line 8a, 8b, 8c, and 8d: Process to Become a Member

Answer "Yes" if you keep records of who is currently a member. If all your members are from the same family, you are not classified as a church. Give IRS the details requested to determine how a person would become a member of your church and what the benefits of that membership are. Attach a copy of an application if one exists.

Line 9: Church Rites and Rituals Performed

These include weddings, baptisms, funerals, and other rites.

Line 10: Religious Instruction

Do you have regularly scheduled youth or children's educational activities such as Sunday school?

Line 11a and 11b: Prescribed Course of Study

What training has your minister or religious leader completed? Self-ordination, self-study, or methods that did not include a formal course of instruction and learning do not qualify as a prescribed course of study.

Line 12: Is Your Religious Leader An Official In Your Church?

If the minister or other religious leader is listed in Part V, Line 1a, check "Yes."

Line 13: Do You Ordain, Commission, Or License Ministers?

If so, include an explanation of the requirements to be ordained, commissioned, or licensed.

Line 14: Are You Part of a Group of Churches With Similar Beliefs and Structures?

Are you part of a convention, association, or union of churches? Include the name of the group you are part of.

Line 15: Do You Issue Church Charters?

If so, what are the requirements for issuing a charter?

Line 16: Fee for Charter

If you paid a fee for a church charter, include a copy of the charter. Be sure to tell which organization provided the charter and their requirements. Do not include organizational charters from the Secretary of State, Franchise Tax Board, or other governmental administrative function.

Line 17: Additional Information

Is there anything else you want IRS to know to decide if you qualify for tax exemption as a church? Attach it to the package or include it in the narrative.

SCHEDULE B: SCHOOLS, COLLEGES, AND UNIVERSITIES

Not all schools are created equal and not all schools qualify for tax exempt status. Your organization is only qualified if your main activity is conducting formal instruction, if you have scheduled habitual customary curriculum, qualified teachers, an identifiable student body who take classes on a regular basis, and there is an identifiable location for these classes and students to meet to conduct this formal, habitual, scheduled curricular instruction. Sounds like a mouthful, but it is the IRS making sure you actually are conducting instruction, not running a diploma mill.

IRS definition of school includes "primary, secondary, preparatory, high schools, colleges, and universities." Home schools do not qualify for tax exempt status.

SECTION I: OPERATIONAL INFORMATION

Lines 1a and 1b: Do You Qualify As a School?

If you can answer "Yes" to both questions, provide requested descriptions in the narrative and move on. If not, you are NOT a school for tax exempt purposes.

Lines 2a and 2b: Are You A Public School? If you can answer "Yes" to both questions, provide requested descriptions in the narrative and move on. If not, do not fill out the rest of Schedule B.

Line 3: Your Location

What is the name of the public school district, and county where you conduct instruction?

Lines 4, 5, and 6: Discriminatory Practices.

These questions seek to determine if you discriminate based on race, color, and national or ethnic origin. If you do, you do not qualify for tax exempt status. Include a copy of your bylaws containing your nondiscrimination policy. If it is not included in your formal organizing or operating documents, include a copy of your signed resolution approving a nondiscrimination policy.

Line 7: Fair Market Value of Services

It is possible that if this applies to your school, you have already answered this question back in Part VIII, question 7. If so, you can reference that answer, but be sure and include any additional information requested that is not included in Part VIII.

Line 8: Who will manage your activities?

If you select "No" be sure to include all required documentation. You can reference Part VIII if you have already provided this information.

SECTION II: ESTABLISHMENT OF RACIALLY NONDISCRIMINATORY POLICY

Revenue Procedure 75-50 requires that you not only have a racial nondiscrimination policy, but that you also publicize it. The statement that must be used is included in quotes in the next paragraph. Revenue Ruling 71-447 clarifies what nondiscrimination means in terms of tax exempt status,

> *"The _____ School admits the students of any race to all the rights, privileges, programs, and activities generally accorded or made available to students at that school and that the school does not discriminate on the basis of race in administration of its educational policies, admissions policies, scholarship and loan programs, and athletic and other school-administered programs."*

In addition, nondiscrimination statements must be included in all brochures, advertisements, catalogs, and other printed materials given to the public and the student body. Don't forget to include it on internet pages. The exact wording IRS likes to see is:

> *"The _____ School admits students of any race, color, and national or ethnic origin."*

Line 1: Do You Have a Nondiscriminatory Policy In Effect?

If you do not, you must approve a resolution implementing one and attach evidence to this application that you have one in place or you will be denied tax exempt status.

Line 2: Is The Nondiscriminatory Policy Publicized In Your Documents?

If "Yes," attach a copy of one of your documents like a brochure or catalog that shows how you are marking your documents. If "No," that means you agree to put the policy in all future documents for the public or student body.

Line 3: Publication in a General Circulation Newspaper

You have to prove to IRS that the public knows you do not discriminate. The easiest way to meet this requirement is to publish the following statement in the newspaper annually. If you have done so, send the entire newspaper page with the application. No partial pages or copies from a copying machine are acceptable. The newspaper disclosure should read:

"The _____ School admits the students of any race to all the rights, privileges, programs, and activities generally accorded or made available to students at that school and that the school does not discriminate on the basis of race in administration of its educational policies, admissions policies, scholarship and loan programs, and athletic and other school-administered programs."

Line 4: Discrimination

If you answer "Yes" to this question, you will be denied 501(c) (3) status.

Line 5: Racial Composition

IRS wants numbers of students, not percentages. Do not include names of staff, faculty, or students, just the actual number (or projected number if you are just starting out) in each category. If you are estimating, you have to submit information explaining to IRS how you came up with the estimates. You can use census data for your area and estimate based on percentages from the census. If your numbers differ significantly from the census data submitted, you have to explain why.

Line 6: Racial Composition for Loans and Scholarships

Use current year actual numbers and projected numbers for next academic year.

Line 7a and 7b: List of Those Who Were Instrumental In Starting The School And Whether They Want To Segregate

For 7a, provide a list of all incorporators, founders, board members, donors of land, and donors of buildings. Then in 7b, explain any circumstance in which any of those listed in 7a has an objective to keep public or private education segregated by race. Schools who promote segregation are not eligible for tax exempt status.

Line 8: Records for Three Years

Revenue Ruling 75-50 requires you to keep specific records if you want to get and keep tax exempt status. You need to maintain records for a minimum of three years showing your school's racial composition, evidence that your scholarships and loans are awarded without discrimination, copies of solicitation materials for contributions, copies of brochures, advertisements, application forms, catalogs, etc. If you plan to do that or are already doing it, answer "Yes." If "No" you must explain how you plan to meet these requirements.

SCHEDULE C: HOSPITALS AND MEDICAL RESEARCH ORGANIZATIONS

If you are a cooperative hospital service organization, you do not need to fill out Schedule C. It is only used if you are a hospital or medical research organization operated in combination with a hospital. If the main function of an organization is medical treatment services, it qualifies as a medical care facility even though it may be operating on an outpatient basis. Treatment can be for physical or mental conditions and includes drug treatment centers.

The definition of hospital does not include convalescent homes, children or elderly homes, or institutions providing job training for the handicapped.

According to IRS guidelines, a medical research organization is one whose "principal purpose or function is the direct, continuous, and active conduct of medical research in conjunction with a hospital." In addition, IRS requires that "the research must be to discover, develop, or verify knowledge relating to the causes, diagnosis, treatment, prevention, or control of human physical or mental diseases and impairments."

Hospitals complete Section I of Schedule C. Medical Research Organizations complete Section II.

SECTION I: HOSPITALS

Line 1: Who Has Staff Privileges?

If all doctors in your area have staff privileges or are only restricted due to capacity, then mark "Yes." If "No," describe how you determine which courtesy staff has privileges at your facility and the exact criteria and selection procedures used.

Lines 2a, 2b, and 2c: Insurance, Self-Pay, Medicare, and Medicaid

If you restrict admission in any of these categories, you must provide an explanation of how and why you restrict patient admittance to exclude any of these categories.

Line 3a and 3b: Medicare/Medicaid Deposits

If you require a deposit, how do you determine the amount, and why do you require it? Is a similar deposit required of patients who do not have Medicare or Medicaid? If not, why not? Describe in detail.

Lines 4a, 4b, and 4c: Emergency Services

What provisions do you have to treat emergencies when someone cannot pay? Do you have a written policy? Do you have written or verbal agreements with first responders concerning emergency services? Describe them and include copies of written policies and agreements. If you have verbal agreements, explain them in detail to include how and when the agreement was made.

Lines 5a, 5b, 5c, 5d, and 5e: Provisions for Charity Patients

Describe in detail how you handle charity patients.

Lines 6a and 6b: Medical Training and Community Education

Include details of how your program works and any organizational affiliations.

Line 7: Office Space to Physicians

If you lease to physicians, you must show IRS that you are getting fair market value for the space and provide representative copies of leases.

Line 8: Governing Boards

This question seeks to ascertain whether your board of directors is representative of the community where you are located. IRS instructions for this item give this exact guidance:

Answer "Yes" if you have a board of directors that is representative of the community you serve. Include a list of each board member with the individual's name and employment affiliation. Also, for each board member, describe how that individual represents the community. Generally, hospital employees and staff physicians are not individuals considered to be community representatives.

Answer "Yes" if an organization described in Section 501(c)(3) with a community board exercises rights or powers over you, such as the right to appoint members to your governing board of directors and the power to approve certain transactions. Describe these rights and powers. In addition, describe how each of that organization's board of directors represents the community.

Answer "Yes" if you are subject to a state corporate practice of medicine law that requires your governing board to be composed solely of physicians licensed to practice medicine in the state. If you answer "Yes" on this basis, also provide the following information.

- Describe whether a hospital described in Section 501(c)(3) exercises any rights or powers over you.
- Identify the corporate practice of medicine law under which you operate.
- Explain how the Section 501(c)(3) hospital exercises any rights or powers over you, such as the right to appoint members to your governing board of directors and the right to approve certain transactions.
- Explain what services you provide to the Section 501(c)(3) hospital.

Line 9: Joint Ventures

Make sure that if you participate in joint ventures, you answer each part of this question and your answers match Part VIII, Line 8.

Line 10: Managing Your Programs

If you contract the management of your programs, provide all requested information and make sure your answers match Part VIII, Line 7b.

Line 11: Physician Recruitment Incentives

It is okay to offer incentives to recruit physicians, especially in shortage areas. Disclose all incentives in detail.

Line 12: Do You Lease From Physicians Who Have a Financial or Professional Relationship With Your Hospital?

This question includes any physician you have a business relationship with: employees, staff physicians, those who are in a joint venture with you, or those you have service contracts with. How did you establish fair market value?

Line 13: Purchase from Business Colleagues

If you purchased an existing medical practice, supplies, equipment, or any other business asset from anyone you had a business relationship with, you must disclose it, and how you established fair market value. Include copies of sales contracts and appraisals.

Line 14: Conflict of Interest Policy

If you do not have one in place, how do you avoid conflicts in business dealings? If you do have one, does it meet or exceed the IRS example? How did you adopt it: bylaws, resolution, etc.?

Having a conflict of interest policy is not required by tax law, but IRS looks at it as one more step to ensure that you are operating to benefit the community and not for private advantage or gain.

SECTION II: MEDICAL RESEARCH ORGANIZATIONS

Line 1: Relationships with Hospitals

Provide a list of all hospitals you work with, describe the nature of the interaction and relationships, and attach copies of all agreements.

Line 2: Schedule of Activities

Whether actual or proposed, provide a schedule of your activities that directly supports your medical research. Include the characteristics and features of the activities and how much money you are spending or will spend on each activity. According to IRS, making grants to other organizations is not an activity of your research.

Line 3: Assets

List your assets, their fair market value, and what percentage of each asset is being used for research.

SCHEDULE D: SECTION 509(A) (3) SUPPORTING ORGANIZATION

If you chose Part IX, line 5d, you have to complete Schedule D because you said you are an organization that only gives money to other nonprofit organizations. This is common when you are a supporting arm of an established tax exempt organization that doesn't want to detract from its nonprofit mission to raise funds. So you are the fundraising body that supports the other organization. This is permissible as long as you maintain control, but several possibilities exist that you may be controlled (in the eyes of IRS) by "disqualified persons."

Electing this schedule has many technical applications, and I strongly suggest you seek the help of a tax professional before filing to eliminate months of follow up paperwork to meet the intent and letter of the law for IRS. The technicalities are beyond the scope of this book. It is a book in itself, and is worth every cent you spend to get a professional to complete this schedule. You may want to go back and see if this is the best selection under Part IX. If another less complicated selection is possible, you may want to choose it.

However, if you are still sure you want to file Schedule D, here is some basic guidance and resources to figure out the technicalities.

If in doubt, contact IRS and talk with them about your specific circumstances before filing.

First of all, you can qualify as a public charity under Section 509(a) (3) if you operate entirely to benefit, perform the functions of, or carry out the purposes of one or more public charities listed in Section 509 (a) (1). This will include organizations who get their funding from a wide range of sources, such as churches, schools, hospitals, etc. You can also qualify as a public charity if you exclusively benefit Section 509(a) (2) organizations, which include organizations that get their funds from grants, donations, or fees for their nonprofit purpose.

You can also qualify as a supporting organization if you are supporting the charitable purposes of 501(c) (4) organizations (civil leagues, social welfare organizations, local associations of employees), 501(c) (5) organizations (labor, agriculture, and horticultural organizations), or 501(c) (6) organizations (business leagues, chambers of commerce, and real estate boards).

You also must meet a relationship test, and not be controlled directly or indirectly by "disqualified persons." Visit www.irs.gov and search for Disqualified Persons as Defined in IRC 4946.

An IRS guidance sheet is available at http://www.irs.gov/pub/irs-tege/509a3_typeiandii_guidesheet.pdf to help you determine if you qualify.

SECTION 1: IDENTIFYING INFORMATION ABOUT SUPPORTING ORGANIZATIONS

Line 1: Organizations You Support

Write the name, address, and employer identification number of every organization you support. Attach another sheet of paper if you have more than will fit in the blanks.

Line 2: Are You Supporting Organizations Under Section 509(a) (1) or 509(a) (2)?

If "Yes" go to Section II, Line 1. If "No," continue this section.

Line 3: Are You Supporting Organizations Under Section 501(c) (4), 501(c) (5), or 501(c) (6)?

These organizations include: Civil leagues, social welfare organizations, local associations of employees. These are 501(c) (4) organizations; Labor, agriculture, and horticultural organizations. These are 501(c) (5) organizations; and Business leagues, chambers of commerce, and real estate boards. These are 501(c) (6) organizations. If so, you need to provide the financial data requested or otherwise explain how they are a public charity under Section 509(a) (1) or 509(a) (2).

SECTION II: RELATIONSHIP WITH SUPPORTED ORGANIZATION(S)—THREE TESTS

According to IRS, a supporting organization must meet at least one of these three tests:

- Test 1: "Operated, supervised, or controlled by" one or more publicly supported organizations, or
- Test 2: "Supervised or controlled in connection with" one or more publicly supported organizations, or
- Test 3: "Operated in connection with" one or more publicly supported organizations.

Line 1: Governing Board or Officers

Test 1 ascertains whether most of the governing board or officers are elected or appointed by the supported organization(s). If "Yes," you must give an explanation of how they are appointed or elected. If "No," go on to the next question.

Line 2: Serving On More Than One Governing Board

Test 2 ascertains whether most of the governing board members also serve on the governing board(s) of the supported organization(s). If "Yes," you must give an explanation of how they are appointed or elected. If "No," go to the next question.

Line 3: Responsiveness Test.

Test 3 ascertains whether you are a trust in which the supported organization(s) can force you give an accounting under state law. If "Yes," explain and provide written proof that the supported organization(s) know they can force you to give them an accounting. Then go to line 5. If "No," go on to the next question.

Lines 4a, 4b, 4c, 4d, and 4e: Alternate Ways to Meet Test 3

These five items are designed to provide an alternate method of qualifying under Test 3. Basically, IRS wants to know the nature and extent of working relationships you maintain with supported organization(s), and how much input they have into your grand procedures, investment decisions, and use of funds. All "Yes" answers require documentation to substantiate.

Line 5: Activities

This line ascertains whether you are operated in connection with supported organization(s). If you conduct activities that would otherwise be carried out by the supported organizations if you did not do them, answer "Yes" and give an explanation and skip the rest of Section II. If "No," continue with Section II.

Lines 6a, 6b, 6c, and 6d: Net Income Distribution

This item provides an alternate way to meet the integral part criteria of Test 3. If you distribute at least 85% of your annual net income to supported organization(s), you may qualify for public charity status. Provide requested explanations and lists. If you answer "No" to 6a, and to line 5, you do not qualify for public charity status. Go back and rethink the status you selected in Part X of Form 1023 to see if another selection is more appropriate.

Lines 7a and 7b: Specifying Supported Organization(s)

Look at your organizational document (Articles of Incorporation for example). Did you name the supported organization(s) in it? If "Yes," give the article and paragraph number and go to Section III. Include requested explanation of relationship(s).

If you cannot answer "Yes," you may want to amend your organizing document unless you can provide evidence of historical or continuing relationship between your organization and the supported organization(s). If you cannot do either, you do not qualify as a public charity. Go back to Part X of Form 1023 and rethink your selection to see if another selection is more appropriate.

SECTION III: ORGANIZATIONAL TEST

Lines 1a and 1b: Supported Organization(s) by Name

If you cannot answer "Yes," you do not qualify for public charity status. If you answered "No," you can go back and change your organizing documents. Otherwise, you do not meet the organizational test. You can still go back and change Part X of Form 1023 and select a different choice for public charity status eliminating the need to do Schedule D.

SECTION IV: DISQUALIFIED PERSON TEST

Lines 1a, 1b, and 1c: Disqualified Persons

Organizations controlled directly or indirectly by disqualified people make the organization ineligible for public charity status. Section 4946 of IRS Code gives the following guidelines on who is a disqualified person:

- Substantial Contributor (normally more than $5,000 a year if that is more than 2% of the total contributions of the previous year)
- Foundation manager (includes officers, directors, and trustees)
- Owner of more than 20% interest in an organization that is a substantial contributor
- Family members. IRS defines family members to include "an individual's spouse, ancestors, lineal descendants, and the spouses of his or her lineal descendants. Also, the legally adopted child of an individual is his or her child within the meaning of this regulation. Internal Revenue Code (IRC) 4946(d) provides that the family of any individual shall include only his spouse, ancestors, children, grandchildren, great grandchildren, and the spouses of children, grandchildren, and great grandchildren... The surviving spouse of a child, grandchild, or great grandchild of a substantial contributor (until remarriage).
- Persons who hold more than a 35% interest
- Government official

CHAPTER 25: PART X

SCHEDULE E: ORGANIZATIONS NOT FILING FORM 1023 WITHIN 27 MONTHS OF FORMATION

"There are only two rules for being successful. One, figure out exactly what you want to do, and two, do it."

—Mario Cuomo

If you have been in existence for more than 27 months, you have some special filing rules as far as effective date of your organization. File Schedule E to determine effective date if you want the effective date to be more than 27 months prior to the application date.

Does the date on Form 1023 meet your organization's needs? If so, do not complete Schedule E. If you need to seek a date prior to 27 months, (for example, you have a donor who needs the tax deduction), then you have to fill out Schedule E and prove to IRS that you meet one of the exceptions to the 27 month filing rules.

Here are the exceptions: churches, gross revenue under $5,000 a year, formed before 1969, or if you can prove you acted in good faith and that if IRS granted the earlier date, it would not prejudice the interests of the government. One way you used to be able to prove good faith was to file the Form 1023 before IRS told you to, although it does not always work anymore.

If it is determined that you do not qualify for 501(c) (3) status from date of formation, you may still qualify for 501(c) (4) status for the dates between formation and filing the Form 1023. Normally donations are not deductible for periods covered under 501(c) (4) status.

Line 1: Churches

You only have to fill out Schedule A. Do not complete Schedule E.

Line 2: Gross Receipts

If your gross receipts are under $5,000 or if you are filing within 90 days of the tax year in which your receipts went over $5,000, you get to stop here and not complete the rest of Schedule E.

Lines 3a, 3b, and 3c: Group Exemption

If you answer "No," go to line 4. If you answer "Yes," it means you were part of a group exemption application or an actual subordinate of another group that has notified you that you will no longer be part of that group. If this applies, IRS wants to know if you are applying within 27 months of either being turned down or 27 months from no longer being part of the group. If you answer "Yes," you get to stop filing out this form, you are done.

Line 4: Created Before October 9, 1969?

If "Yes", you get to stop. You are done filling out Schedule E.

Line 5: Why Didn't You File Within 27 Months?

If you answered "No" to lines 1 – 4, answer ""Yes"" to this questions. You are not eligible for an earlier 501(c) (3) status effective date unless you can provide an explanation to IRS why you did not file, why you did not file in good faith, and how approving the earlier date does not compromise the best interest of the government. This can include relying on a tax professional's advice, IRS guidance given in error, complexities in your circumstances making it difficult to ascertain whether to file, etc. You get to stop on this question.

Line 6a: Advanced Ruling

Notice 1382 eliminated advance ruling. Do not answer.

Line 6b: Changes in Source of Support

If you anticipate changes in sources of support, mark "Yes" and fill out line 7.

Line 7: Two Years Projected Income

If you anticipate changes in your source(s) of support, fill out two year's projected income using this table.

Line 8: Exemption under 501(C) (4) For Periods of Operation Prior To Postmark Of This Application

If you want to apply for Section 501(c) (4) status for the times of operation prior to the postmark of this application, fill out page 1 of IRS Form 1024 and attach to the application. Although donations will not normally be tax deductible, there will be no IRS taxes due from the organization for the periods covered under Section 501(c) (4).

CHAPTER 26:
PART X

SCHEDULES F, G, AND H

"What you do speaks so loudly that I cannot hear what you say."
—Ralph Waldo Emerson

SCHEDULE F: HOMES FOR THE ELDERLY OR HANDICAPPED AND LOW-INCOME HOUSING

Homes for elderly and low income must provide affordable housing to a "significant segment" of elderly, handicapped or low income individuals in the community.

SECTION 1: GENERAL INFORMATION

Line 1: Type of Housing

Describe the type of housing you are providing (i.e.–apartment, condo, co-op, private residence).

Line 2: Application

Provide a copy of the application you use to select tenants.

Line 3: Public Awareness

Explain how you advertise your facilities.

Lines 4a, 4b, 4c, and 4d:

Describe each facility, how many people each accommodates, and whether they are renting or purchasing.

Line 5: Contracts and Agreements

Attach samples of documents used for occupancy.

Line 6: Joint Ventures

Provide details of any joint ventures. Make sure the details agree with Part VIII, line 8.

Line 7: Fair Market Value of Services Contracted

Are you contracting with other organizations for services on these properties? If so, how are you arriving at a fair market value for services? Your answer here must agree with Part VIII, line 7a.

Line 8: Management

Elect whether you will manage your facilities in-house, with volunteers, or with independent contractor(s). Make sure your answer agrees with Part VIII, line 7b.

Line 9: Government Housing Programs

Describe any involvement in state, local, and federal government housing programs.

Line 10: Ownership

Do you own or lease? How did you acquire the property? Copies of all applicable documents need to be attached to the application.

SECTION II: HOMES FOR THE ELDERLY OR HANDICAPPED

Lines 1a and 1b: Who do you provide homes for?

Select which class of individuals (elderly or handicapped or both) you provide housing for. Describe how they qualify and how you select applicants.

Lines 2a, 2b, and 2c: Fees and Affordability

Explain the financial requirements and provide documentation.

Lines 3a and 3b: When Someone Cannot Pay.

What do you do when someone cannot pay?

Line 4: Health Care

Do you have health care arrangements for residents? If so, describe them.

Line 5: Needs of Elderly and Handicapped

Describe how your facilities meet physical (such as grab bars in bathrooms, wide doorways for wheelchairs, etc.), emotional, recreational, social, religious and other needs of the elderly and handicapped.

SECTION III: LOW INCOME HOUSING

Line 1: Low Income Housing

If you provide low income housing, what is the criteria to qualify and how do you make the final selection?

Line 2: Fees In Addition To Rent or Mortgage

Are there any other fees? How are they determined? Give detailed explanation.

Lines 3a and 3b: Is Your Housing Affordable to Low Income Individuals?

Give details and explain restrictions to ensure low income.

Revenue Procedure 96-32, 1996-1 C.B. 717, provides guidelines for providing low-income housing that will be treated as charitable: At least 75% of the units are occupied by low-income tenants, or 40% are occupied by tenants earning not more than 120% of the very low-income levels for the area.

Line 4: Social Services

Do you provide social services to residents? If so, describe the services provided.

SCHEDULE G: SUCCESSORS TO OTHER ORGANIZATIONS

The main reason for this schedule is to make sure that no private benefit to shareholders or individuals occurs when one organization (the predecessor) is taken over by or converted to another organization, even if the predecessor was not a tax exempt organization.

Lines 1a and 1b: Previous Organization For-Profit

Was the previous organization a for-profit organization? If so, give the details of how you came to take it over.

Lines 2a, 2b, 2c, 2d, and 2e: Previous Organization Not-For-Profit

Provide all requested details about previous organization, 501(c) (3) status, and why you took over the organization and its assets. Be detailed and specific.

Line 3: Name, Address, EIN of Previous Organization

Self-explanatory.

Line 4: Who Ran The Previous Organization?

Provide requested information in the table provided. Attach a sheet if necessary to provide complete information.

Line 5: Will Anyone From Previous Organization Be Involved In New Organization?

Provide complete details.

Lines 6a, 6b, and 6c: Assets

If any assets were transferred to the new organization, what were they, how was their worth established, and were there any restrictions on the sale or use of these assets? Include copies of all agreements made.

Line 7: Debt Transfer

Did the new organization take on any debts from the previous organization? If so, give full details.

Line 8: Leases

Provide full disclosure of any lease arrangements the new organization will have for previously-owned equipment with the previous for-profit organization or any of its members, officers, trustees, or directors.

Line 9: Leases

Will the new organization lease any equipment to the previous organization or any of its members, officers, trustees, or directors? Provide full disclosure.

SCHEDULE H: ORGANIZATIONS PROVIDING SCHOLARSHIPS, FELLOWSHIPS, EDUCATIONAL LOANS, OR OTHER EDUCATIONAL GRANTS TO INDIVIDUALS AND PRIVATE FOUNDATIONS REQUESTING ADVANCE APPROVAL OF INDIVIDUAL GRANT PROCEDURES

IRS wants to make sure that any scholarships you give as a tax exempt organization are fair in terms of nondiscrimination, merit or need, and available to an open-ended group instead of a preselected group. The scholarship is tax free to the recipient if he or she is a degree-seeking candidate, and uses the funds for educational expenses that include tuition, fees, books, supplies, and equipment for courses. Acceptable educational expenses do not include room, board, travel, research, clerical help, and equipment not required for a course.

SECTION 1: PUBLIC CHARITIES AND PRIVATE FOUNDATIONS

Lines 1a, 1b, 1c, 1d, 1e, and 1f: Types of Grants and Loans

Provide full explanation of grants, loans, scholarships, etc. provided. Although several items are requested, the most important is the application form for your loan or grant. If you do not have one yet, you can find copies online to use as examples to draft one. Answer each part of this question completely.

Line 2: Case Histories

Do you keep complete records of who got scholarships, grants, loans, etc.? Describe the records you keep. If you do not keep records, you must explain how you will make sure your program meets exempt purposes.

Line 3: Specific Criteria for Eligibility

Who is eligible? What is your criteria?

Line 4a, 4b, 4c, and 4d: Specific Criteria to Select Recipients

How will you select recipients, number of recipients, amount for each recipient, and any requirements (such as grade point average) the recipients must meet.

Line 5: Procedures

How will you award the grant and make sure the requirements have been met?

Line 6: Selection Committee

Who is on the current selection committee, what are the requirements, how do you replace selection committee members?

Line 7: Remaining Unbiased

Are family members of your selection committee eligible? If so, how do you remain unbiased in selection? Private foundations are not allowed to award to disqualified persons.

SECTION II: PRIVATE FOUNDATIONS ONLY

Public charities do not fill out this section. You are done!

CHAPTER 27

COMPLETE FORM 1023

PART XI, USER FEE INFORMATION

"Above all, you want to create something you're proud of."

—Richard Branson

If your financials reflect more than $10,000 average gross receipts per year for four years, the user fee is $850. If the average is less than $10,000, the fee is $400. (See Notice 1382)

When you (meaning an officer, director, or trustee) sign the application, you are certifying that everything you are sending is true, correct and complete to the best of your knowledge.

Remember to enclose the two page checklist on top of your application. Even though it is located at the end of the application, it is placed on top of the application and the check placed on top of it when you put it in the envelope. DO NOT STAPLE the check to the application unless you want to irritate the IRS agent.

PART III

SPECIAL
CIRCUMSTANCES

CHAPTER 28

AUTOMATIC REVOCATION OF 501(C)(3) STATUS

"Success is what comes after you stop making excuses."
—Luis Galarza

Most tax exempt organizations have to file an annual report with IRS. This report is some version of the Form 990, and can be:

- Form 990, Return of Organization Exempt From Income Tax
- Form 990-EZ, Short Return of Organization Exempt From Income Tax
- Form 990-PF, Return of Private Foundation
- Form 990-N, (information e-Postcard)

If you fail to file this return for three consecutive years, on the anniversary of the third due date, IRS takes away or revokes your tax exempt status. This is called Automatic Revocation because the computer does it automatically and you are put on a list of organizations that are no longer tax exempt. That list can be found at www.irs.gov then searching for Automatic Revocation of Exemption List.

If you have been automatically revoked, you must resubmit your entire application (including the required fee) and ask IRS to reinstate your tax exempt status.

BE SURE TO WRITE *"AUTOMATICALLY REVOKED"* AT THE TOP OF THE APPLICATION AND ON THE ENVELOPE.

Details of the reinstatement process are contained in IRS Notice 2011-44 located at http://www.irs.gov/irb/2011-25_IRB/ar10.html

Normally the reinstatement date is the date of the new application to IRS, but there are some exceptions. For the date to be retroactive back to the date of revocation, you must file your application for reinstatement within 15 months of whichever is later:

• The date on the revocation letter from IRS
• The date IRS posted the revocation on their website

In addition, you have to jump through some hoops to get the retroactive date. For example, IRS requires you to submit a request for retroactive reinstatement attached to the Form 1023 that includes:

• A detailed statement of all the facts surrounding repeated failure to file, for the entire three year period as well as for each individual year.
• What circumstances led to continual failure, discovery of failure, and what you did to stop or lessen the consequences of the failure to file.
• You must address what you are doing now to keep this from happening again (you can add the task of filing the appropriate return to the job description of one of the board positions such as secretary or treasurer to make sure it gets done and that there is a responsible person to carry out the task or follow up with a bookkeeper or accountant to see that it is done on time).
• Documentation and evidence of the explanations you gave to get retroactive reinstatement.
• All the missing returns for all the years a return was due (some form of Form 990), including the three years not filed and

the current year if applicable. If in doubt, contact IRS and ask them specifically what returns are due.

- A signed and dated statement from an authorized official (trustee, officer, or director) that says:

    I, (Name), (Title) declare, under penalties of perjury, that I am authorized to sign this request for retroactive reinstatement on behalf of [Name of Organization], and I further declare that I have examined this request for retroactive reinstatement, including the written explanation of all the facts and information pertaining to the claim for reasonable cause and the evidence to substantiate the claim for reasonable cause, and to the best of my knowledge and belief, this request is true, correct, and complete.

- You must provide proof that you "exercised ordinary business care and prudence in determining and attempting to comply with…reporting requirements under Section 6033 for each of the three years, and over the entire three-year period." IRS will consider all your evidence and determine if you meet the Reasonable Cause Standard. Here are some things they consider to give a decision in your favor:

    - If you relied on written information from IRS that was in error
    - Events beyond your control that caused you not be able to file for each of the three years and the three year period as a whole
    - Acting responsibly by taking steps to avoid the failure to file and to keep it from happening in the future by trying to prevent the failure if it was foreseen; removing the problem that caused you not to file as soon as you became aware of the failure to file; putting policies and safeguards in place to make sure it doesn't happen in the future

- A history of complying with filing and other requirements before and after the three year period
- How heavily you rely on volunteers to perform organizational activities also plays a part in the decision making process. The more, the better.

If you want retroactive coverage of tax exempt status, you need to be very thorough in your explanation of what happened and make sure you let IRS know that you did not fail to comply as rebellion against the tax system. You may even want to start your explanation with that statement so IRS gets the idea immediately that you were not being rebellious. You must provide evidence of everything you say to justify the problem, and you must make sure you have instituted safeguards to make sure it never happens again. If your request for retroactive status is turned down, the date of your new Form 1023 filing will be the effective date for tax exempt status.

You will not be revoked a second time unless you fail to file for three years AFTER receiving the new determination letter reinstating your tax exempt status.

CHAPTER 29

INTERACTIVE ONLINE FORM
i1023

"If you cannot do great things, do small things in a great way."
—Napoleon Hill

Over the past several years, articles have appeared on the internet purporting that when the interactive IRS Form i1023 becomes a reality, the process of getting approved for tax exempt status would be simplified and would require much less work. In September, 2013, the Form i1023 was available for review, although the application could not actually be used to file with IRS. I was able to test drive the form and give feedback to IRS. Following is what I found.

The form is available but is pretty much exactly like the paper form and the form available as a fillable form online. IRS put pop-up information boxes throughout the form. The information in the boxes was, in most cases, word-for-word out of the instruction manual for filling out the Form 1023. The only other additions were occasional links to certain IRS publications that give definitions and time saving access to publications.

Unfortunately, the interactive form does not lessen the requirements or speed up processing of the application. In essence, the interactive online Form i1023 is about the same as the fillable form currently available, except for the pop-up boxes with instructions and the links to other publications and parts of the IRS website. You still have to provide in depth narrative explanations and you still have to print and mail.

PART IV

OPTIONAL FOLLOW UP TASKS

CHAPTER 30

REGISTER FOR CHARITABLE FUNDRAISING AND SOLICITATION

"Those who dream by day are cognizant of many things that escape those who only dream by night."

—Edgar Allan Poe

UNIFIED REGISTRATION STATEMENT (URS)

Consumer protection laws exist to ensure that citizens of a state do not fall prey to false charity solicitations. It's so they do not get suckered into parting with their hard-earned money to causes that are not really tax exempt. Many states require nonprofits to register before they are allowed to raise funds in that state. The paperwork, fees, and time frames vary depending on the state, but the Unified Registration Statement (URS) simplifies the process.

The URS is a multi-state registration form that allows your organization to fill it out once, then file it with many states instead of filling out a different form for every state you plan to do fundraising in. Not all states accept the URS (Arizona, Colorado, District of Columbia, Florida, Maine, Ohio, Oklahoma, and South Carolina do not). But many do, either for initial registration, renewal, or both. You can access the form at http://www.multistatefiling.org/ or http://www.multistatefiling.org/urs_webv401.pdf

As of 2014, the following states do not require you to register for fundraising:

> Delaware
> Idaho
> Indiana
> Iowa
> Montana
> Nebraska
> Nevada
> South Dakota
> Texas* (see note below)
> Vermont
> Wyoming

*   Texas requires registration for law enforcement, public safety, and veteran causes only.

Each state has its own requirements, fees, and filing procedures. Many adhere to the Charleston Principles to determine if a tax exempt organization should file if they have only minimal financial dealings within a state or may access donors by internet only. States are not bound by these principles and set their own rules of who has to register. The Charleston Principles can be viewed online at the Association of Fundraising Professionals website, or by just searching for Charleston Principles.

For information on fundraising registration requirements for every state, visit www.doyourownnonprofit.com and click on the *Helpful Links* tab.

CHAPTER 31

ANNUAL FILING REQUIREMENTS WITH IRS

"I learned that courage is not the absence of fear, but the triumph over it."

—Nelson Mandela

REPORTS TO FILE

The IRS gives you tax exempt status, but with conditions. You must report to them annually (with very limited exceptions) about the income and expenses of the nonprofit organization. The form used to report depends on the status of the organization in terms of revenue, assets, and/or type of nonprofit. The smaller you are, the less you have to report. In most cases, if your income is less than $50,000, you do not even have to give an exact amount.

If you are a church or subordinate auxiliary of a church, you have no reporting requirements. However, many churches choose to report voluntarily to create transparency and keep everything on the up and up. Other organizations that do not have to file annual reports include state institutions and organizations that fall under parent organizations and qualify as auxiliary organizations of the parent, as well as nonprofit organizations that have not been officially approved by IRS for tax exempt status yet. When in doubt, call IRS and ask. The number is 877-829-5500.

If you fail to file the required form for three years, your tax exempt status will be automatically revoked on the due date of the report for the third year. At that time, you must reapply for tax exempt status and pay the fee all over again, except that you must justify the reason for not filing (for each year you didn't file and for the entire time of failure to file). Consider assigning the responsibility of completing the required returns to a specific position on the board of directors or board of trustees so that it gets done on time every year. The person holding the assigned position should be responsible to report the progress, the completion, or problems to the board concerning the required filings.

The reports you file with IRS are public record except that the name of the donors and the amount of their contributions is not public record. When filing, leave off social security numbers and other identifying information for the officers, directors, trustees and other officials because the information given in the return is public.

Filing consists of completing some version of the IRS Form 990. The versions are similar to the Form 1040 taxpayers file in that there is a long form (Form 1040), short form (Form 1040A), and the simple uncomplicated form (Form 1040EZ). You can look at a copy of the various Forms 990 and review the required information at www.irs. gov then search for Current Form 990 Series–Forms and Instructions.

The available versions for tax exempt organizations are:

FORM 990

RETURN OF ORGANIZATION EXEMPT FROM INCOME TAX

This is the long form that must be filed if an organization's assets are over $500,000 or their income is over $200,000. It applies to all Section 501(c), 527, or 4947(a)(1) organizations except black lung benefit trusts and private foundations. The long form is similar to a tax return for an individual with a business. Just like an individual tax return, not everything on the form applies to everyone filing a return. Also, depending on the nature of the business, extra schedules may be required to be included with the return. A nonprofit organization may be required to file extra schedules depending on the nature of the nonprofit endeavors, interaction with other organizations, types of fundraising, political activity, compensation, operations outside the United States, etc.

FORM 990-EZ

SHORT FORM RETURN OF ORGANIZATION EXEMPT FROM INCOME TAX

This is the short form that may be filed if an organization's assets are under $500,000 and their income is less than $200,000. The exceptions are sponsoring organizations of donor-advised funds, organizations that operate one or more hospital facilities, and certain controlling organizations defined in Section 512(b)(13). They must file Form 990.

FORM 990-N

E-POSTCARD

Most smaller organizations with tax exempt status and income under $50,000 can file the Form 990-N, but can also file the Form 990-EZ or Form 990 if desired. IRS contracts with Urban Institute to process electronic e-postcard information returns. To file, go to http://epostcard.form990.org/ and set up an account online. This return is very easy to complete and requires only a few pieces of information: legal name (and any other names used) and address of organization, employer ID number, tax year, name and address of a principal officer, website address if you have one, confirmation that income is less than $50,000, and notification in the case that an organization is going out of business. This return does not require divulging the income of the organization, except that it is under $50,000. The e-postcard can be completed and filing done in less than 10 minutes per year. With such a minimal effort required for small organizations to stay IRS-compliant, there are few good reasons to be revoked for not filing every year.

FORM 990-PF

RETURN OF PRIVATE FOUNDATION

Section 4947(a)(1) trusts are treated as a private foundations. Private foundations are not the focus of this book.

If you need help with filling out the forms or figuring out which form to file, you can call IRS at 1-877-829-5500, or the Help Desk if you are filing electronically at 1-866-255-0654. IRS has provided Urban Institute as their agent for online processing of Form 990-N at no charge to you. If you want to file electronically and cannot or do not choose to file Form 990-N (e-postcard), you can hire an IRS approved firm to file on your behalf. A list of authorized e-file providers is located at http://www.irs.gov/uac/Exempt-Organizations-electronic-filings-(returns-and-notices)

WHERE TO SEND TAX EXEMPT RETURNS

For organizations within the United States, returns are normally sent to:

Department of the Treasury
Internal Revenue Service Center
Ogden, UT 84201-0027

For organizations with principal business office outside the United States, returns are normally sent to:

Internal Revenue Service Center
P.O. Box 409101
Ogden, UT 84409

WHEN TO FILE TAX EXEMPT RETURN

The filing deadline with IRS depends on the fiscal year of the organization. Filing is required by the 15th day of the 5th month after the end of the fiscal year. There are two extensions possible, just like for individual income tax returns, except that the nonprofit extensions are 90 days each.

If an organization's fiscal year ends December 31, their Form 990, 990-EZ, 990-PF, or 990-N is due by May 15th of the following year. The first extension for Form 990, 990-EZ, or 990-PF is until August 15, and the second extension is until November 15th. No extensions are given for Form 990-N. To get an extension, you must file IRS Form 8868, Request for Extension of Time to File an Exempt Organization Return. The form is located at www.irs.gov then search for Form 8868.

CHAPTER 32

APPLY FOR NONPROFIT STANDARD MAIL RATES

"Nobody ever drowned in his own sweat."

—Ann Landers

Once you have nonprofit status with IRS, you may be able to get a nonprofit standard mail rate with the United States Postal Service. Eligible nonprofit organizations include: religious, educational, scientific, philanthropic (charitable), agricultural, labor, veterans, and fraternal.

A responsible official from your organization must fill out United States Postal Service (USPS) PS Form 3624, Application to Mail at Nonprofit Standard Mailing Rates. You can get the form online or you can get a copy of it at the post office. There will be some documents required to submit with the application.

More information is contained in USPS Publication 417. You can view a copy online by searching for USPS Publication 417.

Taking the time to get approved for nonprofit mailings can save a bunch on postage. The post office will weigh one item in your bundle of exact mailings and multiply by the number of items you are mailing. The rate is lower if you use a barcode on your mailing pieces and if they can be processed by machine instead of by hand. Talk with the post office about how to secure your newsletters or other mail pieces.

If you use staples to close a newsletter, your newsletters get torn in processing, and can prohibit machining the mailing. Tape and postal seals work better and save on postage because they can be processed as machinable mail, saving significantly on every item.

It's best to talk with the postal workers who will actually process your nonprofit mailings before you send any out. They can give you all the discount information and all the requirements so you get your mailing ready correctly the first time, and show you examples of properly prepared bulk nonprofit mailings.

SUMMARY

I hope this book has helped you navigate the sometimes tricky waters of government procedure and bureaucracy at state and federal levels. These rules and requirements exist to safeguard the public from fraud and scams, but for those of us who are hardworking honest people, it may seem like overkill. Granted, applying for 501(c) (3) may not have been the easiest thing you ever did, but think about the result, the good you will do in the future because you completed the process now. I think you will agree it was worth the effort!

I have tried to make the whole 501(c) (3) process simple from idea to reality by providing step by step guidance, attorney prepared templates of required state documents, and links to the paperwork for approved organizations. I am also willing to answer specific questions for you as you go through the process. Please feel free to contact me at any time for additional help. You might also want to go to www. doyourownnonprofit.com and review our forums and blog, or join our mailing list for periodic free reports and updates on the 501(c) (3) process. We will not bombard you with constant emails, but will occasionally touch base with information and tips for starting, running, or getting funding for your nonprofit.

May God richly bless your efforts!

APPENDIX A

ACTUAL APPROVED NONPROFIT APPLICATIONS

NO NEED TO REINVENT THE WHEEL

One of the best parts of starting a nonprofit corporation is that you do not have to reinvent the wheel. If you know of a similar organization, you can request a copy of their Form 1023 with narrative. Wording on applications is not copyrighted and if you see something you can use, tweak it to fit your organization instead of starting from scratch. Don't make it any harder than necessary.

I have included many actual approved nonprofit applications to help you get through the process. If you see one in this list that's similar to your organization, go to the website and review the application. All links worked at the time of publication. Links are also live at www.doyourownnonprofit.com

Some packages given are Form 1023 prior to the June, 2006 revision of the form, but the information is similar and those that contain the narratives are very helpful in understanding the kinds of information IRS wants to know to approve your application. I attempted to include a variety of nonprofits including religious, historical, medical, educational, and sports organizations, charitable trusts, and animal shelters. I also included an older Form 1023 for a farmer's market that failed the first attempt with IRS but includes some helpful insight into the process of how to fix applications if they are not correct the first time.

The budget information ranges from $0 for brand new nonprofits just starting, up to budgets of hundreds of thousands of dollars. These are included to give you a broad range of examples. In addition, many also include their organizing documents and bylaws. Those organizational documents that contain the determination letter or other correspondence from IRS have been added after IRS completed their application. Your paperwork will not have those until IRS sends them after the fact.

NOTE: These links all worked at the time of publication. For live links, visit www.doyourownnonprofit.com

● ● ●

A Great Example of a 2004 Completed Application with Narrative Sections particularly well done for Trolleyride.org (Minnesota Streetcar Museum):

Minnesota Street Car Museum, Inc.:

http://www.trolleyride.org/Member_stuff1/IRS_Documents/1023/IRS_Form_1023.pdf

http://www.trolleyride.org/Member_stuff1/IRS_Documents/1023/Narrative.pdf

http://www.trolleyride.org/Member_stuff1/IRS_Documents/1023/Attachment_D.pdf

http://www.trolleyride.org/Member_stuff1/IRS_Documents/1023/Attachment_B.pdf

http://www.trolleyride.org/Member_stuff1/IRS_Documents/1023/Attachment_C.pdf

SOME APPLICATIONS THAT
CONTAIN GREAT NARRATIVES:

New Hampshire Supreme Court Society:

> http://www.nhsupremecourtsociety.org/1023.pdf

Friends of the Trumbull High School Choir, Inc.:

> http://www.fothsci.org/uploads/5/2/4/9/5249683/fothsci_
> form_1023_application_for_recognition_of_exemption_-_501c3.
> pdf

The HAMS Harm Reduction Network, Incorporated:

> http://hamsnetwork.org/corporate/f1023.pdf

Friends of Niger:

> http://www.friendsofniger.org/pdf/FONTaxExemptApp.pdf

Beaumont Charitable Foundation:

> http://www.ci.beaumont.ca.us/DocumentCenter/Home/
> View/3076

Cape Elizabeth Education Foundation:

> http://www.ceef.us/storage/downloadable-docs/01%2005%20
> 17%20501c3%20Application%20-%20IRS%20Form%201023.pdf

LegalCORPS:

> http://legalcorps.org/wp-content/uploads/2012/01/1023-
> PubInspCopy.pdf

Sandasarana Children's Educational Fund, c/o Saint Philip the Apostle Church:

http://www.sceflanka.org/pdfs/notification/Form%201023%20petition.pdf

Minnesota Groundwater Association Foundation:

http://www.mgwa.org/foundation/documents/mgwaf-irs-1023.pdf

United Way of Metropolitan Chicago:

http://uw-mc.org/wp-content/uploads/2008/11/UWMC-IRS-Exemption-Application-1023.pdf

Statement Arts, Inc.:

http://statementarts.org/files/Statement_Arts_1023.pdf

The Clear Fund:

http://www.givewell.org/files/ClearFund/Clear%20Fund%20Form%201023.pdf

Denver Early Childhood Council:

http://www.denverearlychildhood.org/pdf/1023%20FINAL%20without%20addendums.pdf

Miller & Zois Kids Foundation, Inc.:

http://www.millerzoiskidsfoundation.com/PDF/MillerZoisKids.pdf

Equipped to Survive Foundation, Inc.:

http://www.equipped.com/etsfi_form1023.pdf

The Light Millennium, Inc.:

http://www.lightmillennium.org/501_c_3/lmtv_form_1023.pdf

Television, Internet, & Video Association of DC, Inc.:

http://www.tivadc.org/Resources/Documents/TIVA_
Form_1023_final_093009forweb.pdf

USA Projects:

http://www.unitedstatesartists.org/pdf/USA_Projects_
Form_1023.pdf

Wycliffe Bible Translators International, Inc.:

http://resources.wycliffe.net/financials/WBTI_1023_Application.
PDF

Software Freedom Conservancy, Inc.:

http://sfconservancy.org/docs/conservancy_Form-1023.pdf

Fort Bend County Sheriffs Employees Charitable Foundation:

http://www.behindthebadgecharities.org/IRS%20Application%20
for%20Exemption%20complete%20file.pdf

Rocky Mountain Foundation of Hope:

http://www.rockymountainhope.org/_wp/wp-content/
uploads/2010/01/RMFH%20Form%201023.pdf

The Seniors Intervention Group Inc.:

http://seniorsinterventiongroup.org/app/SIG-501-c-3-Final-Signed.pdf

Arizona Center for Investigative Journalism, Inc.:

http://arizonawatch.org/wp-content/uploads/2012/08/Final-1023.pdf

Prairie Gold Homes, Inc.:

http://www.prairiegoldhomes.org/downloads/IRSApplication.pdf

1by1 International, Inc.:

http://static.squarespace.com/static/51da06bfe4b0108eefe2761b/t/51f79c54e4b0dcb625417bec/1375181908106/1023.pdf

DuPont Circle Village, Inc.:

http://www.dupontcirclevillage.org/Documents/DupontVillageForm1023-Final.pdf

A Grain of Hope Foundation, Inc.:

http://www.agrainofhope.org/form1023.shtml

Your Town Alabama, Inc.:

http://www.yourtownalabama.com/wp-content/uploads/2013/07/IRS-1023-Application-for-Recognition-of-Exemption.pdf

Playa del Fuego, Inc.:

http://playadelfuego.org/sites/default/files/boddocs/IRS-1023-complete.pdf

A few Medical 1023s:

Maine General (several Form 1023 organizations):

http://www.mainegeneral.org/body.cfm?id=1557

San Francisco Free Clinic:

http://www.sffc.org/SFFC_Form_1023_09_09_93.PDF

OTHER APPLICATIONS THAT GIVE A WIDER RANGE OF NONPROFIT EXAMPLES:

The Creek Bed Foundation, a Charitable Trust:

http://thecreekbedfoundation.org/CreekBed1023.pdf

San Diego Speculative Fiction Society, Inc.:

http://www.sansfis.org/corporate_documents/IRS-1023/sansfis_irs1023.pdf

National Consortium for College Completion, Inc.:

http://www.completecollege.org/docs/Form%201023.pdf

New Mexico GLBTQ Centers:

https://secure.nmag.gov/coros/Documents/26-2022345%5CIRS TaxExemptApplication(Form1023).pdf

Hands N Feet Foundation:

http://www.handsnfeetfoundation.org/wp-content/uploads/2012/08/form1023.pdf

Husky Swimming Foundation (Also shows good wording to expedite application):

http://www.huskyswimmingfoundation.com/wp-content/HSF_Form1023.pdf

Shoe Giver of Tampa, Inc.:

http://shoegiveroftampa.org/pdfs/Shoe-Giver-Application.pdf

The Cordoba Initiative:

http://www.investigativeproject.org/documents/misc/435.pdf

Blount County Humane Society:

http://www.blountcountyhumanesociety.org/PDFs/BCHS%201023.pdf

Gaskov Clerge Foundation (GCF):

http://www.gaskov.org/Documents/Completed%20990%20Forms/GCF501C3%20%20%20501c3.pdf

Society of King Charles the Martyr, Inc.:

http://www.skcm-usa.org/Legal/SKCMForm1023asFiled.pdf

One with Christ Ministries, Inc.:

http://www.onewithchristministries.org/tax-exempt-501-c-3/ irs-form-1023/

Shenango Chapter NAVHDA, Inc.:

http://www.shenangonavhda.com/501_c__3__Application.pdf

Vial of Life Project:

http://www.vialoflife.com/images/Application%20for%20501-c-3.pdf

Grandfather Mountain Stewardship Foundation, Inc.:

http://www.grandfather.com/wp-content/uploads/2011/06/ Application-for-Recognition-of-Exemption-Under-Section-501c3.pdf

Continuation Fund, Inc.:

http://antiochcollege.org/sites/default/files/docs/Continuation_ Fund-1023_Applicatio.pdf

Rural Investment Corporation:

http://www.cfra.org/sites/www.cfra.org/files/RIC_Application_ for_Recognition_of_Exemption_1023.pdf

Mozilla Foundation:

http://static.mozilla.com/foundation/documents/mf-irs-501c3-application-form-1023.pdf

National Council of Young Men's Christian Associations of the United States of America (the original application for YMCA from 1982):

http://www.ymca.net/sites/default/files/organizational-profile/form_1023.pdf

National Council of Nonprofit Association:

http://www.councilofnonprofits.org/files/Form%201023.pdf

The Jackson Foundation:

http://www.thejacksonfoundation.org/Form1023.pdf

Cadasil Together We Have Hope Non-Profit Organization:

http://cadasilfoundation.net/1023%20Original%20%20Application%20for%20Website.pdf

Dianetics Foundation International:

http://www.xenu-directory.net/documents/corporate/irs/1993-1023-dfi.pdf

Wayland Public Schools Parent Teacher Organization, Inc.:

http://waylandpto.org/wp-content/uploads/2012/08/Form-1023.pdf

Multiple Sclerosis Foundation, Inc.:

http://990online.com/docs/5/592792934_87_1023.pdf

CAIRN Rescue USA:

http://www.cairnrescueusa.com/docs/CRUSA_1023.pdf

Servicemembers Legal Defense Network:

http://sldn.3cdn.net/dd620a17021183177b_jem6iv9px.pdf

Thunderridge Grizzly Bear Backer Club:

http://thunderridge.coloradosportscastnetwork.com/GBBC/
forms/1023%20Application%20for%20Exemption%20
smaller%20file.pdf

Saint Martin's Hospitality Center:

http://www.smhc-nm.org/wp-content/uploads/2012/05/Form-
1023.pdf

The Seti League, Inc.:

http://www.setileague.org/finances/1023.pdf

Napa Emergency Women's Services:

http://www.napanews.org/assets/upload/Form_1023.pdf

The Putnam County Foundation, Inc.:

http://www.pcfoundation.org/documents/PCCFForm1023.pdf

National Foundation for the Centers for Disease Control and Prevention, Inc.:

http://www.cdcfoundation.org/sites/default/files/upload/pdf/
Form1023.pdf

Partner in Health, Inc.:

http://partnerforsurgery.org/wp-content/uploads/2013/03/Form-1023.pdf

The Endeavor Initiative, Inc.:

http://share.endeavor.org/financial/1023%20Form.pdf

Quixote Humane Incorporated:

http://www.quixotehumane.org/501c3/Quixote_Humane_Form_1023.pdf

The Marie A. Dornhecker Charitable Trust:

http://www.dornheckerfoundation.org/Documents/ct_1023.pdf

United States Australian Football League, Inc.:

https://usafl.com/files/USAFL%20Form%201023%20Exemption%20Application.PDF

The Columbia Historical Foundation:

http://www.columbiahistoricalsociety.org/chs_irs_1023_form_093084.pdf

Internet Corporation for Assigned Names and Numbers:

http://archive.icann.org/en/financials/tax/us/form1023.htm

Stegall Charitable Educational Foundation (also includes Form 990s):

http://foundationcenter.org/grantmaker/stegall/appexempt.pdf

Investigative Project on Terrorism Foundation:

http://www.tennessean.com/assets/pdf/DN1658741022.PDF

Malin Bergquist Charities Inc.:

http://www.mbcharities.org/documents/IRSForm1023-Filed2010.pdf

Longer Life Foundation:

http://www.longerlife.org/form_1023.pdf

The Doris M. Carter Family Foundation:

http://carterfamilyfoundation.org/home/images/stories/Treasury-Form-1023.pdf

TALX Charitable Foundation:

http://www.talx.com/aboutus/1023.pdf

Austin Browncoats:

http://www.austinbrowncoats.com/docs/ABC_1023.pdf

The CarMax Foundation:

http://www.carmax.com/assets/xckxeqcxxizfediqz5c5e5lav5ewx5of/form%201023-application%20for%20recognition%20of%20exemption-090308.pdf

Trinity Mission Works, Inc.:

http://www.trinitymissionworks.org/Documents/IRS%20 1023%20ap.pdf

United Way of Southwest Louisiana Community Foundation:

https://www.foundationswla.org/swla/Portals/12/docs/Financial/ IRS%201023%20Application.pdf

Louisiana Hiking Trails, Inc.:

http://louisianahikingtrails.org/about/tax-exempt/1023.pdf

Friendship Academy of Fine Arts Charter School:

http://www.friendshipacademy.org/wp-content/uploads/2012/12/ form_1023_.pdf

Maplewood Memorial Library Foundation:

http://maplewoodlibraryfoundation.files.wordpress.com/2013/07/ application-for-501c3-status.pdf

Moldova Mosaic Foundation:

http://moldovamosaic.org/mmorg/wp-content/uploads/2011/02/ Form-1023-web.pdf

OLDER BUT GOOD FUNDRAISING EXPLANATION:

Nautilus of America, Inc.:

http://oldsite.nautilus.org/admin/taxform-1023.PDF

OLDER BUT GOOD WORDING TO SUPPORT THEIR FUNCTION:

Southwestern Foundation:

  http://www.southwestern.edu/live/files/1234-irs-form-1023

NO FORM 1023, BUT GOOD NARRATIVE SECTION WORTHY OF INCLUDING:

Angels Above Foundation:

  http://www.aaf-epmo.org/AngelsAbove/Assets/aaf-documents/501C3_Appl_Narative.pdf

Greater Tulsa Health Access Network:

  http://greaterthan.securespsites.com/Shared%20Documents/Governing%20Documents/Form%201023%20Attachments.pdf

San Francisco-Krakow Cities Association:

  http://www.polishclubsf.org/Summary.pdf

Friends of Olympia Farmer's Market (turned down the first attempt, but fixed the application and then approved. Shows application and IRS correspondence):

  http://www.farmers-market.org/wp-content/uploads/2012/10/Application-of-Exemption.pdf

JOINT VENTURE FUNDRAISING

If your organization needs to raise money consider holding a joint fundraiser with Pasture Valley Children Missions.

We purchase handmade jewelry from the Bambanani Project in Nhlangano, Swaziland, made by older orphans at Pasture Valley Children's Home, and women in the community. The necklaces, bracelets, and earrings are made from paper beads that have been rolled tightly and varnished. Some are also made of seeds. I have worn the same favorite necklaces for several years and they have held up perfectly as they are made with great pride and quality.

Marielle DeJong (right) and friend at Pasture Valley Children's Home

In addition, you can order laminated bookmarks made from local plants in Swaziland, decorated by hand, with your organization info and logo on the back. Very impressive but very reasonable. Buy for $1, sell for $2.50, or give away to your supporters.

HOW IT WORKS

You tell us how many necklaces you want and what sizes (short fits most people), medium, long, and extra-long (wraps at least twice around the neck). We also have bracelets and earrings and can get matching sets in requested colors. There are other crafts available as well: purses, passport bags, etc.

You deposit half the retail cost of the jewelry plus shipping, either by check from you or your organization. Then you hold your sale. It is an easy way to raise $500-$1,500 quickly. We suggest a price of double the wholesale price you purchase for, but you can charge whatever you wish at your sale. Small group sales where people have time to try on the jewelry with no pressure produces great sales.

If you sell it all, you keep what you collected, we keep the deposit. If you do not sell it all, we will refund the portion of your deposit for the amount of jewelry you return to us in the same condition you received it. You have no risk of unsold merchandise.

The half we collect goes right back into the Bambanani Project so that we have funds available to purchase more jewelry. We have worked with several organizations and all have been happy: Tri-County Independent Living, Phelps R-III school district in Salem, Missouri to help fund space camp for 10 of their students, USA Athletes International to name just a few. These items sell well to church groups, women's clubs, and in schools.

You can also purchase directly from the Bambanani Project by going to http://pasturevalley.com/the-bambanani-project/

Contact us at: support@pasturevalleychildren.com
or visit www.pasturevalleychildren.com

Host 501c3 Workshop

Host a Tax Exempt 501(c) (3) Nonprofit Workshop in your area!
If several people in your area have ideas for nonprofits, but need help getting it all together, why not host a workshop at a local school, college, church, or even a weekend retreat? It can be a fun, relaxed time of getting past the confusing paperwork and starting something great.

Dr. Kitty Bickford is available to do 1 or 2 day workshops providing hands-on training for the entire 501(c) (3) application process from idea to reality. Bring your idea, roll up your sleeves, and by the end of the workshop, all the red tape will be done and you will have created an organization ready to submit for 501(c) (3) status.

To Schedule:

Email me at:
workshops@doyourownnonprofit.com

ORDER FORM

Attorney-Prepared
Fill-in-the-Blank Templates
For Required State Documents

Name _____

Address _____

City _____ St _____ Zip_____

Phone _____

Email my order to:

_____

Fill out reverse side and mail payment to:

Chalfant Eckert Publishing
1028 S. Bishop Avenue, Dept. 178
Rolla, MO 65401

For Credit Card Orders with immediate email delivery:

www.doyourownnonprofit.com

I would like to order documents for _____ (state or DC)

_____ Certificate of Formation in Word format $9.95
_____ Bylaws in Word format $9.95
_____ Articles and Bylaws with FREE BONUSES $19.95
        Includes these 3 FREE Templates:
        Conflict of Interest Policy
        Annual Conflict Statement
        Initial Board Meeting Minutes

        Total enclosed   _____

Thank you for your order. We hope it saves you much time and effort in getting 501(c) (3) status.

Note: If you need a different format, please email us at support@doyourownnonprofit.com and we will try to accommodate your request.

Note from the Publisher

Are you a first time author?

Not sure how to proceed to get your book published?
Want to keep all your rights and all your royalties?
Want it to look as good as a Top 10 publisher?
Need help with editing, layout, cover design?
Want it out there selling in 90 days or less?

Visit our website for some exciting new options!

www.chalfant-eckert-publishing.com

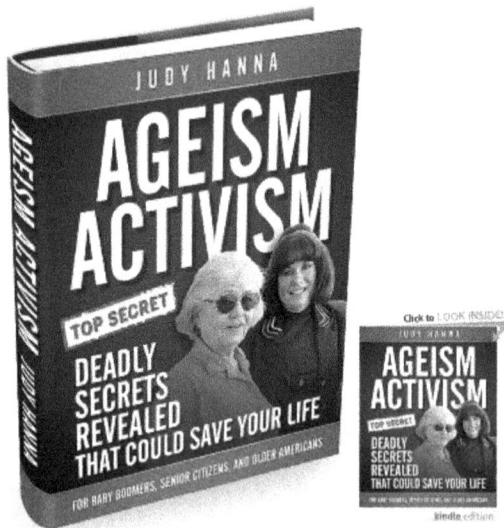

www.ingramcontent.com/pod-product-compliance
Lightning Source LLC
Chambersburg PA
CBHW051948090426
42741CB00008B/1311